Overcoming The Attack Of The Jezebel Spirit

The Church Under Siege

By

Don Richter

Endorsements

Over the past few years there has been much teaching and preaching on the Jezebel spirit. **This manifestation of the spirit of control and seduction is often seen in the highest echelons of the ministry.** *Though much has been taught, not as much has presented a balanced view of this serious but fixable problem in the church.* **Thankfully, my friend, Don Richter, has brought a balanced and beneficial teaching** *that can help individuals discern the diabolical strategy of the enemy, and assist churches to effectively live in liberty from the harassment of this long-term enemy of leadership in the church.*

> **Stan E. DeKoven, Ph.D., MFT**, President,
> Vision International Education Network,
> Vision International University
> Ramona, CA

In **Overcoming the Attack of the Jezebel Spirit,** *Don Richter brings a balanced, pastoral approach and understanding to this church epidemic. While theologians may differ on what to call it, this spirit is all too familiar in the church and must be exposed and dealt with effectively. With love and compassion,* **Don masterfully defines the problem,**

offers real-life illustrations, Biblical references, and practical pastoral advice. Pastors and parishioners alike will benefit from the related and relevant church issues addressed in this book.
>   **Dr. Phil Derstine, Sr. Pastor**
>   President Christian Retreat
>   Gospel Crusade, Inc.
>   Bradenton, FL

Overcoming the Attack of the Jezebel Spirit *is a guide into an otherwise darkened path of feelings and reactions. It will help to bring discerning of spirits before devastation can occur.* **Don Richter has authored some fresh insights** *into a subject that for many has been veiled and has, as a result, led to pain. It is a book for pastors and their leaders alike.*
>   **Bernard Evans**
>   President, Elim Fellowship
>   Lima, NY

Overcoming the Attack of the Jezebel Spirit *is an excellent resource for defining, identifying, and overcoming a persistent and dangerous threat to the church. There is not a pastor or church leader who has not experienced the pain and frustration caused by the "Jezebel spirit." In order to overcome, you need to know your enemy!* **This book looks at every aspect of the attack and, more importantly, gives strategies for victory.**
>   **Dr. Victor Torres, Sr. Pastor**
>   Reach Out
>   Family Worship Center
>   Hyde Park, NY

I find **Overcoming the Attack of the Jezebel Spirit** *very well written and easy to read, with the development of the theme being clear and insightful.* **The big "plus"** *is that it is*

actually a manual for pastors, to help them see what is happening in their churches and to show the way to uncovering the Jezebelic activity and deal with it. **This is an excellent leadership tool.**
> **Dr. Fount Shults**
> President, On Word Ministries
> Myrtle Beach, SC

The apostle Paul said, "We are not ignorant of the devil's devices." **Overcoming the Attack of the Jezebel Spirit** *gives new insights on an age-old problem. A church leader will learn to recognize the deceptive influences that are designed to control and mislead him. Don Richter, with his long experience in pastoring and overseas ministry, writes from personal experience on this very prevalent but still unrecognized challenge. It is a must-read for serious leaders.*
> **Rev. Paul Johansson**
> President, Elim Bible Institute
> Lima, NY

Overcoming the Attack of the Jezebel Spirit *is a God-appointed message that needs to be heralded throughout the church. Don Richter does a stellar job exposing the destructive, deceptive nature of the Jezebel spirit within the local church and the devastation it leaves in its wake. This book is not only a treatise on tactics used by the enemy of your soul, but* **the author also instructs with keen biblical insight on** *"overcoming the attack of the Jezebel spirit"... before it's too late!*
> **Michael DiNardo, Sr. Pastor**
> New Creation Christian Church
> Newburgh, NY

Don Richter is a man of God with an extraordinary ability to blend his many years of ministry experience with sound Biblical teaching. This combination produces a uniquely detailed and balanced teaching on the Jezebel spirit. **Overcoming the Attack of the Jezebel Spirit** *clearly presents to the reader the signs and symptoms of this bothersome spirit, as well as practical ways to use our God-given authority to disengage its power.* **Truly this is a spiritual handbook that is a must for every pastor's desk.**

> **Rev. Carol Missik, Sr. Pastor**
> Living Word Church
> Hermitage, PA

Don Richter has hit a home run with his book, **Overcoming the Attack of the Jezebel Spirit.** *It should be required reading for every person who is called to pastoral ministry. This book unveils the source behind much of the division, disunity, and discouragement in the church that pastors and leaders must deal with.*

> **Charles F. Hamilton, Sr. Pastor**
> The Upper Room Fellowship
> Columbiana, OH

The only way to win a battle is to know the strategies of the enemy. *Don has been on the frontlines for many years and has discovered that* **the spirit of Jezebel is one of the most often used strategies of the devil** *to divide and destroy the Body of Christ. Every leader in the church needs to read* **Overcoming the Attack of the Jezebel Spirit** *to understand and avoid the pitfalls of the spirit of Jezebel.*

> **Oscar Nuncio**
> Leadership Seminar Coordinator
> Harvest Preparation
> International Ministries
> Sarasota, FL

Don Richter did an outstanding job—what a great book!
He has identified the enemy within. I realize the enemy can
use each of us. Having had this knowledge available when I
began as a pastor would have given me such good insight to
understanding people. This book not only tells us how the
enemy works, but it also tells how to identify and stop the
enemy before his attack destroys the church.
Reuben Beachy
Pastor, Conservative
Mennonite Conference
Sarasota, FL

Overcoming the Attack of the Jezebel Spirit *by Don*
Richter is an eye-opening book speaking of an issue that
most are unwilling to approach. This attack is recognized
as a primary foe in the battlefield of ministry. Don's careful
analysis and powerful insights leave the reader, especially
those in leadership, with tools to gently and firmly minister
victoriously in the heat of the attack of the Jezebel spirit.
The truths contained in this book will enable leaders and
members alike to walk in the awareness and discernment
required, while approaching the matter compassionately. I
recommend this book to you.
Dale E. Haight, Sr. Pastor
Praise Fellowship
Russell, PA

It is good to see that there is still a watchman on the wall for
the church and her leaders. Don Richter's work,
Overcoming the Attack of the Jezebel Spirit, *should be*
required reading for any pastor or member of a new
church work. The Jezebel spirit is a vicious spiritual enemy
that has devoured and ruined many of God's shepherds.
Don Richter has given us a tool to withstand its assault and
experience the victory God intends for His church. This

Holy Spirit-directed manual will reveal the plans formed against us and give confidence that we can be overcomers. As one who has lived through this ungodly assault, I recommend this book as a truthful, powerful tool.
A.J. Baisch, Sr. Pastor
New Harvest Church
Myrtle Beach, SC

Don Richter's book, **Overcoming the Attack of the Jezebel Spirit,** *written from a place of study, prayer, and experience, adds insight to what many have written on this subject.* **This spirit is a true threat to the church of Jesus Christ, but it will not prevail as long as we have men of God like Don to give insight and direction.** *This book is more than a good read. It is a manual to help pastors, elders, and leaders recognize this spirit before it gains a foothold; this book will give understanding to help overcome this spirit's intended attack. I believe this book is a must-read for all those in ministry and training for ministry. As Don has said, "* **Standing in a place of neutrality opens the door for the Jezebelic attack.***"*
Ralph Diaz, Sr. Pastor
New Harvest Christian Church
Newburgh, NY

I have just finished reading **Overcoming the Attack of the Jezebel Spirit,** *and I highly recommend that this book be in every pastor's library.* **It would also be a great book for every church member to use for personal study and in small group settings.** *It is written in a very clear and concise style. Especially helpful to me was* **the chapter on the operation of the Jezebel spirit; also, the chapter on**

God's vision for the church gave me an even greater love and appreciation for the local church.
Shirley Stryffeler
Upper Room Fellowship
Columbiana, OH

Overcoming the Attack of the Jezebel Spirit *is a book that every pastor, worship leader, elder, and layperson should be reading and re-reading. It's not only a book with an important warfare strategy for the church but also a* **book that will bring encouragement and hope to the body of Christ.** *If you are looking for a resource that will help you recognize, defuse, and defeat the plans of the enemy as well as bring healing and restoration to the people of God, this book is it.*
Chip Richter, Director
RPM PRODUCTIONS
"Music for Kids and Families"
Columbiana, OH

Rev. Don Richter is a person that I consider a true father in the faith, and I count it a privilege to call him my friend. I **applaud him for writing a book that brings clarity to a highly misunderstood subject.** *The revelation and life experience that he brings prove to make this a classic handbook for any person who is serious about defeating the most common attack against the church.* **This book will enlighten the novice and bring answers to the experienced.** *As such, I* **recommend that every pastor (for that matter, every Christian)** *who is wholehearted about building the kingdom of God should have this book in his or her arsenal.*
Stephen Schlabach, Sr. Pastor
Shining Light Bible Church
Sarasota, FL

I have known Pastor Don as a "father in the faith" and can say with enthusiasm that **Overcoming the Attack of the Jezebel Spirit** *is a labor of his love that overflows from his heart for the Lord and for the church of Jesus Christ. Any* **church member, ministry leader, pastor, or other leader, has either experienced, or will experience, the devastating influence that "the Jezebel spirit"** *has on the Body of Christ. Read – no!* **— Consume this book,** *as it is written by a man with a deep care for you and for God's church.*

> **Jack Hempfling, Sr. Pastor**
> Living Waters Church
> Leroy, NY

Few books provide a useful addition to the pastor's toolbox that will prevent confusion and a loss of momentum affecting God's purpose and ongoing vision for the local church. Pastor Don Richter provides a precision tool to do just that in **Overcoming the Attack of the Jezebel Spirit.** *Not only did I find it insightful and personally challenging, I recommend it as a "must-read" for any pastor who wants to stay on course and prevent a crippling attack of the enemy wrapped in this despicable guise. Pastor Don gives us a "telescope" that will allow us to see this attack coming long before it is allowed to do any damage to the people we love.*

> **Rick Smail Sr. Pastor**
> City Church
> Philadelphia, PA

I know of no other man who I would deem more qualified to bring such a message to the body of Christ. *Don Richter carries an apostolic mantle on his life that is both authoritative and at the same time very gentle. The wisdom of his years as a spiritual father shines through on these pages and gives clear understanding to anyone who has an ear to hear. I would recommend* **Overcoming the Attack of the**

Jezebel Spirit *to any pastor or leader in the church world, whether he is a young man just stepping into the fray or a more mature man who has experienced the ferocity of the battle. Either way* **this book will provide valuable insights to you and enable you to say along with the apostle Paul** *"we are not unaware of our adversary's devices."*
> **Randy Thurman, Sr. Pastor**
> Kingdom Life Church
> Fort Myers, FL

Some months ago my good friend Don Richter sent me a copy of his new book, **Overcoming the Attack of the Jezebel Spirit.** *My initial response to the book was, "Oh, no. Not another one of these!" Down through the years I had been given various writings on the Jezebel spirit—invariably all dealing with outspoken and troublesome sisters in the church. "Jezebel" had, consequently, become one of my least favorite subjects. Then Don called me and asked me for some publishable thoughts about his book. I now had to read the manuscript!*

I read most of the book in one sitting, and I was overwhelmed by Don's insights! It was as if he were recounting what we ourselves, as a congregation, had walked through just a few short years ago. As Don defined the origins and the activities of the Jezebel spirit and **then outlined the ways in which we can identify and then deal with that spirit** *in the church and how* **the Body of Christ can be recovered from its effects,** *I felt as if his book was a personal prophetic word to me, to my family, to our leadership and to our whole congregation in the aftermath of our own struggles.*

I personally saw afresh the seriousness of walking above reproach in the ministry, giving no occasion for the accusations of an accusing enemy; and I saw clearly how to identify and how to deal with that insidious spirit that seeks to overthrow the purposes of God within a local congregation. **Don's work with various Hebrew and Greek words is scholarly; his observations and recommendations are invaluable.** *It is a privilege to commend his book to the Body of Christ to place in its armory for the day of battle.*

We live in momentous days, as Satan seeks every way possible to cripple the Bride of Christ so that she fails in her mission, but our destiny is to triumph through Him who has so loved us, and **Don's book is a great help along the way toward that end!**

> **Charles P. Schmitt, Sr. Pastor**
> Immanuel's Church
> Silver Spring, MD

Don - thank you for giving us a well-rounded view on the influence and activity of the Jezebelic spirit in the church. After reading this book, I found myself asking the Lord to deal with the vulnerabilities in myself that could succumb to Jezebelic activity or serve as a conduit for the same. Speaking as both a pastor under-shepherd and a man seeking God in my own life, you have served the Body of Christ well with this book. Thank you.

> **Pat Burden, Sr. Pastor**
> Mid Hudson Christian Church
> Wallkill, NY

Dedication

This book is dedicated to my wife, Lois, God's gift to me
and to the church. She has faithfully walked in ministry
with me, always carrying more than her load.
Her wisdom— bathed in love and encouragement—
has been an anchor to the lives she touches.

She has truly become the wind beneath my wings.

Table of Contents

Acknowledgments

I could not have finished this book without the love and encouragement of my wife and partner in ministry, Lois, who has contributed greatly to its writing. She has been my greatest sounding board while working out the concepts I have communicated. She also served as a pre-editor, more than once reading every word on every page, preparing the manuscript for final editing. A man is strengthened by his family relationships and that is my testimony as well. My three sons, their wives, and my grandchildren are an ever-increasing source of joy. Their love and support is an encouragement to all I do in life.

My special thanks to those who unselfishly gave of their time to read and respond to the manuscript. Your input has caused this book to be a better work in terms of clarity and readability. I want to acknowledge the staff of Xulon Press, especially the editors who did the final edit of the manuscript. Their skill and dedication has made the book most readable and enjoyable.

I also want to acknowledge and thank my valued friends Paul Johansson, Dr. Dale Fife, Dr Fount Shults, and Dr. Ed Bez, all of whom read this work with pad in hand to critique the theological content.

I thank each of you who prayed diligently for the completion of this book. In that light I acknowledge in particular, Shirley Stryffeler, whose friendship and commitment to prayer has been a great blessing to the kingdom of God and to me personally.

I also acknowledge and honor our precious brothers and sisters who faithfully walk through the very real attack of the Jezebel spirit in the church. You have been an inspiration to me as I have seen your courage and servanthood in the kingdom of God.

Foreword

The church, since its inception, has been crippled and often rendered ineffective by the insidious, persistent attacks of the enemy. We have resisted like boxers throwing punches at shadows, never clearly identifying our actual opponent. Consequently, we have failed to overcome his strategies. Like the "Star Wars" episodes, we know Darth Vader exists and that he is wreaking havoc in the galaxies; we're just not sure about his true identity until the last episode (which happens to be the *prequel*, not the *sequel*).

As I sat on my back porch reading Don Richter's manuscript for the first time, I found myself experiencing what I call the "Aha!" moment. Suddenly, the phantom enemy came into view with startling clarity. "Why didn't I see this before?" I asked myself. "It would have saved me so much grief and frustration as a pastor and leader. Praise God; help has finally arrived!"

Knowledge should not just sit in our heads like money collecting interest. Information and insight is meant to be shared for the good of all. We owe a debt of gratitude to my trusted colleague and dear friend. He has dared to share his knowledge with us for our good! After years of personal combat against the adversary in the local church, he has gathered his accumulated experience into a usable, pragmatic strategy that exposes the despotic Jezebel spirit that has plagued us!

Regardless of what you have thought in the past in terms of spiritual warfare, get ready for revelatory insight. Like an expert, seasoned coach, Don leads us through each chapter of *Overcoming the Attack of the Jezebel Spirit* with the skill of a qualified mentor. He identifies and exposes the enemy with crystalline clarity. But he understands that gaining this knowledge is not enough in and of itself. It is just the first step toward victory. What do we do with what we have learned?

New information demands a new response, not blind adherence to preconceptions. Don moves us from the imbalanced ineffectiveness of past efforts to a new, power-packed, liberating response to the enemy's tactics. With straightforward advice, a line of attack is laid out that, in my opinion, was formulated in the strategy room of heaven. This practical approach can be applied in every setting. It will not only defeat the enemy but keep him on the run as well.

With the affection of a spiritual father's heart and the passion of one called to train and equip pastors and leaders around the world, Don brings his experience and wisdom to the church that he loves, in the name of the Lord Jesus Christ whom he serves with unselfish obedience and integrity.

You may be inundated with things to do; your schedule may be filled to the max. But, reading this book should be a top priority! You may already be the victim of a church split. You might be one of the walking wounded ones who is still feeling the acute pain inflicted by the attack of a fellow Christian. If you are a pastor, leader or Christian, don't delay another minute. This book will prepare you to strike a **"knockout blow"** to the enemy of your soul. I can hear it now: "Aha! So that's what I've been up against."

Thanks Don, for your unflinching courage, superb insight, and practical wisdom.

Dr. Dale A. Fife, Founding Pastor
The Potter's House Church, Farmington, Connecticut
www.tphct.com
Speaker and Author:
The Secret Place, Passionately Pursuing His Presence
The Hidden Kingdom, Journey into the Heart of God

INTRODUCTION

A Prophetic Dream

The deep ruts in the old road caused me to know that others had made this same journey before me. I traveled along, not knowing my destination, and the warmth of the sun streaming through the leaves felt good in the spring air. I was aware of the need to walk carefully to avoid the potholes and obstacles along the way. The air was warming quickly as the sun rose above the trees. I was naïve, with a sense of confidence and wellbeing flooding my soul, as I successfully negotiated my way over the well-traveled route. I was totally focused on the task at hand, to move along this road, which obviously had guided so many who traveled before me.

Enjoying my journey, I came upon a bank-style barn with weathered siding. This kind of barn is very common in areas where flat land is scarce and thus two-story barns are built into the hillside with the top floor extended out to provide a run-in shelter for animals. A rail fence just a few feet off the road marked the boundaries of the barnyard, which contained a mix of sheep and male deer. The barnyard was filled to capacity, with the animals pressed against one another. They were just standing still rather than moving around, and they seemed to be staring at me as I approached. My pace slowed and my attention was drawn to what initially appeared to be a fruitful, prosperous herd of animals. My impression soon turned to horror as my mind digested what I was seeing .

Some of the sheep had fresh wounds where chunks of flesh were torn from their bodies. Studying the flock I saw that each of the sheep had been wounded to some degree. Some wounds were so severe they appeared to be life threatening. It was evident that some of the wounds were fresh; I saw blood flowing from gaping flesh. The thought that the deer, with their sharp antlers, must be responsible for the damage was soon dispelled by what I observed. Some of the sheep, first appearing the same as the others, soon took on a new appearance to me as I realized they stood with chunks of flesh and wool hanging from their mouths! Horror mixed with grief dominated my senses and was intensified by the smell of rotting flesh reaching my nostrils. My heart was filled with compassion and an urgency to come to their aid.

I turned from the road at the corner of the fence and a few quick steps brought me to the gate of the barnyard. As I approached the wooden gate, I noticed it was in excellent shape, well maintained and carefully constructed for strength and durability. The top of the gate, an inverted arch, came just above my waist. When I paused to consider what course of action to take, a man stepped from the shadow cast by the shelter of the bank barn. As he approached the gate, I could sense the evil that surrounded his presence. He was dressed in black, including a large, black cape. A black, wide-brimmed felt hat topped off his overall menacing appearance. He said nothing, but his posture and position clearly communicated his intent to prevent me from entering the barnyard. He stopped and stood a few inches from the other side of the gate. My mind began to evaluate the situation, to formulate a strategy to defeat this opposing force, which intended to keep me from entering. My hands rested on the grips of two western-style revolvers that were loaded and ready for action. Realizing that the wooden gate would serve to hide my hand movement, the element of surprise was on my side. With one swift, sure movement the revolvers cleared the holsters. In the blink of an eye, bullets crashed through the gate with thundering accuracy, finding their mark with devastating intent. After discharging every round in the chambers, a sense of desperation set in as the menacing figure, seemingly unaffected by my attack, reached across the fence and wrapped his arms around my upper body with fierce strength. Dropping my guns, my hands found a firm grip at the base of his chin, which was as high as my forehead. I pushed with all of my strength in an effort to break the crushing hold that seemed to intensify as we struggled. I felt movement and realized that his face had come off in my hands, thus revealing another face. Each time I grappled with him another face appeared. Deep within my spirit the knowledge rose that no power in heaven or on earth is greater than the name of Jesus. My ears heard my voice, before my mind finished realizing what was needed: **"In Jesus' name, in Jesus' name, in Jesus' name!"**

I awoke, realizing that I had been dreaming. But, the knowledge that it was a dream did nothing to calm my troubled soul. I knew instantly, in my spirit, that I had experienced a prophetic dream.

When I experienced this dream, I shared it with the congregation I was pastoring. As time unfolded I realized the Holy Spirit was speaking to me to be on guard for the sake of these people God had called me to care for. I have since come to know that this prophetic dream was relevant for that time and place as well as for what I would be doing in the future.

After 31 years of ministry, I now recognize the greater significance and importance of the dream and how it relates to the life of the church. The road traveled by so many represents the road others in ministry have traveled over the years. The mix of sheep and deer represented the people in the church. The deer, with their antlers, looked menacing, appearing guilty of the vicious attacks. However, it was the sheep that were responsible for devastating one another. I understand that the dream is a clear picture of how the Jezebel spirit attacks the church, using sheep to wound and devour one another. The figure from the darkness represented a demonic figure assigned to oversee the attack. His job was to stop anything that would interfere with the progress of the attack. He remained hidden until I made a move to rescue the sheep from themselves. He only appeared when their sabotage was going to be stopped. My initial attempt was to deal with this force by fleshly means, represented by the guns I had in my hands. In desperation I continued to move in my own ability, only now the attack was directed at me. I felt as though my very life was draining from my body as my strength gave way to this overwhelming force. It seemed hopeless as I called upon Jesus, the Name above all names.

The fact that I awoke before seeing the ending troubled me for a while, but as I prayed and meditated on the dream, I realized that God wanted me to see the end of the dream, not in my sleep, but wide awake as He led me through the inevitable attack of the Jezebel spirit.

Answering His call to serve Him as a leader in the church has given me the opportunity to know His faithfulness. The passage telling us He will never leave us nor forsake us is His promise to us who are facing the challenges in the church. The gates of hell will not prevail against the church. To God be the glory.

Now to Him who is able to do exceedingly abundantly above all that we ask or think, according to the power that works in us, to Him be glory in the church by Christ Jesus to all generations, forever and ever. Amen.

Ephesians 3:20-21

CHAPTER ONE

The Jezebel Spirit: "Real or Myth?"

See then that you walk circumspectly, not as
fools but as wise,

Ephesians 5:15

Is the Jezebel spirit real or a myth? This is a very important question, and the only way to approach the answer is to consider what the scriptures say about the Jezebel spirit. We also need to consider why and how the church uses this term to express what we experience as a very real attack against the purposes of God. I recall the day I was first introduced to the idea of the Jezebel spirit. I had just begun to pastor and was keenly interested in all that would help in the care of God's people. A woman of our congregation brought up the subject of the Jezebel spirit. I never heard or considered that such a spirit existed. Her words were enough to pique my interest in determining its validity.

My decision to write this book was based on conclusions I have come to regarding the reality of "Jezebelic activity" in the church. I wish I'd had a book such as this in my hands when the subject came up at that early point of my pastorate. I'm convinced I did not handle things as well as I would have if I'd had a mature understanding of this attack on the church and had known how to identify and stand against it. I read a book by Dutch Sheets called *Intercessory Prayer*, which I highly recommend. He made two statements that confirmed to me the need to write this book. He said, "If you don't know what you're looking for, you probably won't find it;" and, "If you don't know how to do what you are doing, you probably won't do it very well." I have found both of these statements to be true in my life and ministry.

Balance Is a Virtue

I am not hyper-mystical when it comes to supernatural activity in the church. It is an obvious fact that both God and Satan are involved in the activity in the church. A mature position to have concerning demons, evil spirits and their activity in the life of the church, is one of balance. Some people have a tendency to bring a focus to the activity of Satan rather than to the victory we have in Christ Jesus. This is very damaging to the purposes of God. We need to respond appropriately to Him and to the attack of the enemy.

Stopping Short Is Costly

As my search began for the definition and understanding of the term "Jezebel spirit" I turned to the Scripture, where I found no direct reference to "the Jezebel spirit." However, I did find references to Jezebel, the wife of Ahab (a king of Israel). This caused me some concern and I did not pursue this study very far at the time. I have since concluded that was a mistake! Over the years I came to know that it not only exists, but sometimes it is glamorized to the point of spiritual distraction. My goal is to validate and expose the activity of the attack against the church without bringing glamour or glory to it, staying focused on the victory we have in Christ Jesus. I do not want to stop short as I embrace God's design for the church to succeed. It would be too costly!

Definition Brings Clarity

What are we saying when we use the term "the Jezebel spirit?" I have heard a variety of implications in the use of the term. Often, subsequent conversations reveal very little biblically-based, theological understanding; instead, they reveal an experience-based theology, which lacks the necessary foundation for ongoing growth and maturity.

I think it is important, for the purpose of this book, to express clearly what I am saying when I use the term. In brief, Jezebelic activity in the church is Satan's use of man's carnal nature to bring the church to the place of being dysfunctional. You will find more detailed insight into the definition and the origins of the Jezebelic attack in Chapters Two and Three.

Biblical Integrity

In order to achieve understanding that brings growth and maturity, it is important that the necessary biblical foundation relative to the Jezebel spirit be established.

There is clear biblical integrity for the use of the term "the Jezebel spirit." A study of scripture reveals very interesting insights into the use of the term, as well as validating the reality and nature of the attack by the Jezebel spirit. We cannot find the exact expression "Jezebel spirit" in the Bible. However, we do find scripture that builds foundation for the use of the term in both the Old and New Testaments.

When we look for the name Jezebel in Scripture, we find it is used twenty times, once in the New Testament and nineteen times in the Old Testament.

Old Testament

In the Old Testament, the word Jezebel is the translation of the Hebrew word 'Iyzebel;[1] Izebel, the wife of king Ahab. This word appears nineteen times in 1st and 2nd Kings. All of these passages refer to the wife of Ahab, the King.

> In the thirty-eighth year of Asa king of Judah, Ahab the son of Omri became king over Israel; and Ahab the son of Omri reigned over Israel in Samaria twenty-two years. Now Ahab the son of Omri did evil in the sight of the LORD, more than all who were before him.
>
> And it came to pass, as though it had been a trivial thing for him to walk in the sins of Jeroboam the son of Nebat, that he took as wife Jezebel the daughter of Ethbaal, king of the Sidonians; and he went and served Baal and worshiped him.
>
> 1 Kings 16:29-31

New Testament

In the New Testament the word Jezebel is the translation of the word Iezabel; [2] Jezabel (i.e., Jezebel) a Tyrian woman, used as a synonym of a false teacher [termagant]. This word appears once in Revelation 2:20 as Jesus is addressing the Church in Thyatira.

> Nevertheless I have a few things against you, because you allow that woman Jezebel, who calls herself a prophetess, to teach and seduce My servants to commit sexual immorality and eat things sacrificed to idols.
>
> Revelation 2:20

In this passage Jesus uses the words "that woman Jezebel" to describe ungodly activity that is being tolerated in the church unnecessarily.

We have been given every spiritual blessing in heavenly realms to deal effectively with ungodliness in our midst.

> Blessed be the God and Father of our Lord Jesus Christ, who has blessed us with every spiritual blessing in the heavenly places in Christ, just as He chose us in Him before the foundation of the world, that we should be holy and without blame before Him in love.
>
> Ephesians 1:3-4

The church can choose to tolerate such activity, but to do so is without excuse.

The Use of the Term "Jezebel Spirit"

Jesus is not referring to an individual named Jezebel, but rather the character demonstrated by the person Jezebel. The Scriptures reveal the characteristics of the person Jezebel in the Old Testament. We see these characteristics surrounding the attack of Satan that has become so familiar to every local church.

Based on these identifying characteristics, we have legitimized a name for this attack: "the Jezebel spirit." It is very important for us to discover the foundation needed for a well thought out, balanced answer when we are responding to people who are questioning the validity of the term "the Jezebel spirit."

Our response must be established on a biblically-based foundation to enable understanding that leads to maturity. A response seasoned with understanding and wisdom will help us avoid being brought to a place of being ineffective when dealing with Jezebelic activity in the church.

So Here Is the Dilemma

The Pitfall of Neutrality

As a pastor, I have been guilty of not dealing aggressively with the attack of the Jezebel spirit in the local church. I judged those who came to me with an unbalanced approach in dealing with this attack as though they were suffering from toxic spirituality. On the other hand, I heard others say, "If I can't find it in Scripture, it does not exist." I agree it is necessary for Scripture to confirm what we do and say as people of God. However, embracing either one of these extremes will position us in a place of not dealing with the issue.

When we are in a place of not embracing either position, we are in a place of neutrality. Standing in a place of neutrality opens the door for the Jezebelic attack. As we will find out in this book, the attack can be devastating. The church can be brought to the place of being dysfunctional, unable to accomplish God's purposes. We must do everything we can to prevent that from happening.

What Is the Proper Response?

If we respond poorly to the question "Real or Myth" we position the church to fail. Unfortunately, too often that has been the case. The responsibility of leadership is to equip the church to be victorious. When leadership fails to do that, the church is less effective in dealing with the destructive, devastating attack we have come to know as "the Jezebel spirit."

Because of the stigma of appearing too mystical, some pastors write off the idea of Jezebelic activity in the church, not supporting any effort to combat such. In some cases, leadership in the church becomes very silent on this topic in order to avoid the criticism of appearing to give too much attention to the attack.

What has been your response to the attack and the term "the Jezebel spirit?" Have you written it off as hyper-spiritual or non-existent? Have you become silent so as not to draw attention to it? If you have, your neutrality may have given place to this devastating attack in the church, nullifying God's anointing and purpose that His church should be set apart to accomplish His will.

The proper response must be to proactively embrace the challenge to understand and to address the issues surrounding the topic and the attack of the Jezebel spirit.

A Balanced Proactive Approach

Presenting a balanced approach in dealing with Jezebelic activity requires insight and understanding without bringing undue attention to the reality of Jezebelic activity in the local church. History and experience would indicate the attack is inevitable. God's design for the church includes specific elements which, when embraced, overcome the attack before it gets a foothold.

The devastation that is experienced by local congregations through Jezebelic activity is also a part of our history. If we are equipped with a strategy ahead of time, we can effectively stop the devastation that previously has taken its toll over and over again in the local church.

You Can Overcome the Attack of the Jezebel Spirit

You can be used and abused by Jezebelic activity in the church. God knew you would face the challenge of this attack from the beginning of time. He has established His church with forethought and design for victory. If you embrace God's design, you will overcome. God has set in place a church that is equipped to be overcomers, and that is who you are.

Jezebelic activity is neither a myth nor is it nonexistent. We must deal with the reality of the church under siege from this hideous attack and then embrace the challenge that will prove us to be overcomers.

CHAPTER TWO

The Assignment of the Jezebel Spirit

He opened his mouth to blaspheme God, and to slander his name and his dwelling place and those who live in heaven.

Revelation 13:6 NIV

It was early morning and I could not sleep. My night had been a restless time. I lay in bed considering all the details of the ministry.

This has been a long night! I thought. *Once again the work of the ministry is at a standstill. Why does this keep happening? It seems as though every time we make some progress the challenges get even greater. I wish there were peace in the house of God. There is an elders' meeting tonight, and I already sense strife in my spirit. These men seem to live to aggravate one another. They have taken their relationship to a new level, called relating by our carnal nature. "God help us!"*

Two more people have removed themselves from leadership positions. I've been told it is my fault because I just burn people out. The worship leader resigned again, the third time this year. The intercessors just told me that I don't hear God anymore. God, I wonder if I ever did hear You.

The intercessors also announced that the angels who had stood guard over the property have left. Because of this report we have ten more empty seats on Sunday morning. Two more people are threatening to leave because the angels are no longer watching over the property. The marriage-counseling load is more than I can handle. The youth pastors have stopped coming to church. My wife has been injured by the criticism that seems to flow non-stop in our direction.

My mind had been so overloaded recently that I was late leaving to do a funeral, and now the family feels that I do not consider their needs to be important. Let me tell you, it is better to be late for your own funeral than to be a pastor and arrive late for the funeral of someone else!

Maybe that is not such a bad idea ... my own funeral. It sure would make a lot of people in the church happier. Oh yes, and speaking of my own funeral, what about that letter I was given by one of the women in the church that her husband wrote. He states in the letter how he intends to kill me, and it's written with a very detailed, graphic description. This is more than a person should endure!

The church finances are a challenge. Our biggest tithers have withdrawn their financial support. They have announced that they are not going anywhere, but until I change some things around here, the money stops. It is time to review the budget, and somehow God's intent is that we make this work. Our church treasurer calls me a spendthrift and has decided to stand against me so that my supposed wasteful and reckless spending doesn't bankrupt the church. He has said (but not to me directly, of course) that he feels solely responsible for the financial success of the ministry.

Now my family doesn't want to attend church any more,

but I put my foot down which brought resolution to this problem. It did require us to compromise our positions. They have agreed to attend church, just not the one I pastor. I didn't tell them that I honestly don't want to attend this church either.

Well, I've just been accused of lying and deceiving the flock. I'm now told I'm the world's worst communicator and that all these confused people whom I pastor are evidence of that fact. You know, I never knew ministry would be like this.

I can't believe it; another pastor who I know has had moral failure. At least they have identified his failure as moral. With me it's not so specific;, I'm just an overall failure. I just heard that some are saying I have lost my anointing, whatever that is. Sometimes I wonder if I ever had it. As a matter of fact, I wonder if I ever should have entered the ministry. I seem to be doing more harm than good. I know He said, "feed my sheep." Sheep ... I don't think He meant for the pastor to be what the sheep devour. It is pretty hard to feed sheep that are attacking one another and you as well.

Maybe I should resign and let someone who has " the anointing" take my place. I should talk this over, but... with who?

Yes, I think God is trying to tell me something. I wish I could just get away to hear Him, but that is not going to happen. There seems to be a move afoot to keep track of my time and ministry. The elders are using my secretary to find out how I spend my time. They are convinced that with so many problems in the church, I must be a slacker.

It has been rumored that I am so busy with things in the church that I have lost my focus in caring for the people. Someone said I didn't return a call. I learned they never called in the first place. I asked why they said I never returned the call that they never made. They said, "Well, perhaps I shouldn't have said it, but I know how busy you are, and if I had called, you would not have returned my call."

I realize that God's call on my life to serve as a pastor in His church has reached a place of not accomplishing what He has intended.

The bright sun is coming in the window. I can't sleep. I might as well get up. Lord, help me face another day.

The Work of the Jezebel Spirit Is Covert

Does all this sound a little unreal? It is more real than you might think. These experiences are common to pastors and leaders who are serving God in the church. The problem is that so many times we do not recognize the work of the Jezebel spirit in what we call the "negative things" that happen to people, and especially to those who are serving in ministry in local churches. But not all of these experiences are just "negative" things.

It is a great problem when we don't recognize the work of the Jezebel spirit in our midst. The reason for this oversight is the covert nature of Jezebelic activity. Not identifying Jezebelic activity has a devastating effect in the church. God help us to see more clearly.

The Assignment of the Jezebel Spirit

In order to have a clear understanding of the assignment of the Jezebel spirit, it is necessary for us to take a look at the objective of the Jezebelic attack from a biblical perspective.

The Objective

The apparent objective of the attack of the Jezebel spirit is to stop the purposes of God from being realized by those who He has anointed to participate in His purposes.

When we trace history back to the earliest evidence of this attack, we find it in the book of Genesis. Here we find the account not only of the creation of man but also the fall of man, which resulted in man not fulfilling God's purposes.

Then God said, "Let us make man in our image, in our likeness, and let them rule over the fish of the sea and the birds of the air, over the livestock, over all the earth, and over all the creatures that move along the ground." So God created man in his own image, in the image of God he created him; male and female he created them.

God blessed them and said to them, "Be fruitful and increase in number; fill the earth and subdue it. Rule over the fish of the sea and the birds of thc air and over every living creature that moves on the ground."

Genesis 1: 26-28

God's Purpose in Creation

To understand God's purpose it is necessary to look at this passage as a prophetic word of what was to come. We understand that the prophetic deals with the present and the future, often at the same time. I see this passage as one such scripture. God is giving a clear vision of man's purpose and function. Man was created in His image and released to multiply, subdue, and rule.

What we are seeing in this passage is the first phase of His plan to bring forth the bride (His church). It is the bride who will ultimately be in His image and rule with Him for eternity. God had a vision for the bride before He spoke and created. The bride was not an afterthought. He has designed His creation so that His vision for the bride will become a reality.

Truly the purpose of God is to see the reality of the bride. This infuriates Satan, because the bride will be all that Satan aspired to be through his own limited power.

"How you are fallen from heaven, O Lucifer, son of the morning! How you are cut down to the ground, you who weakened the nations! For you have said in your heart: 'I will ascend into heaven, I will exalt my throne above the stars of God; I will also sit on the mount of the congregation on the farthest sides of the north; I will ascend above the heights of the clouds, I will be like the Most High.' Yet you shall be brought down to Sheol, to the lowest depths of the Pit.

Isaiah 14:12-15

Not only will the bride fully be all those things Satan aspired to be, but she also becomes one with the Lord. Satan is committed to do all that he can to stop this from happening.

Satan Enters the Picture

He comes to steal, to kill, and to destroy. In this next portion of Scripture it tells how he seeks to destroy the process that will result in the vision of God for the bride to be manifest.

Now the serpent was more cunning than any beast of the field which the LORD God had made. And he said to the woman, "Has God indeed said, 'You shall not eat of every tree of the garden'?" And the woman said to the serpent, "We may eat the fruit of the trees of the garden; but of the fruit of the tree which is in the midst of the garden, God has said, 'You shall not eat it, nor shall you touch it, lest you die.' " Then the serpent said to the woman, "You will not surely die. For God knows that in the day you eat of it your eyes will be opened, and you will be like God, knowing good and evil."

So when the woman saw that the tree was
good for food, that it was pleasant to the eyes,
and a tree desirable to make one wise, she took
of its fruit and ate. She also gave to her husband
with her, and he ate. Then the eyes of both of
them were opened, and they knew that they
were naked; and they sewed fig leaves together
and made themselves coverings.

Genesis 3:1-7

Satan Appeals to Our Carnal Nature

Satan's approach with Adam and Eve was to appeal to
their "carnal nature." He approached Eve with what
appealed to her intellect, ambition, and understanding.
The tree appeared pleasing to the eye, was good for food,
and was desirable to make her wise, so she made a choice;
this choice was not based on the eternal purpose of God,
but on her finite understanding, motivated by the confidence of her flesh. She then offered to Adam what was
forbidden, and he too entered into the tragic — yet anticipated — fall of man.

They could have made their decision based on a love
relationship with God, embracing their Creator and His
vision, submitting to His authority in their lives. This would
have led them to the destiny God had planned for them.

The documentation of the fall of man reveals the weakness of our flesh and the hideous nature of Satan. Here is the
first evidence in Scripture that reveals the basic strategy of
Satan. He chooses the flesh of man to influence the process
of God's purpose for creation, which is to bring forth His
true church, the bride.

Jezebelic activity in the Old Testament was rooted in the
flesh. The strategy was, and is, to take advantage of the
weaknesses of our flesh, which is constantly seeking self-
satisfaction. The weakness of our flesh becomes powerful in

the hands of God's enemy, Satan, who is also the enemy of our soul.

The Bride Manifest

The purpose of God as it relates to us is to see that the process of the manifestation of the bride goes forward. God's plan for that to happen is in seeing His fullness being established on the face of the earth through His church, His body. We recognize that the manifestation of the bride is a process God set in place from the beginning of time. The whole intent of Scripture is to reveal God and His purposes in the creation of man and his ultimate destiny.

The Bride in the Book of Revelation

We see the bride as John sees the bride in this fantastic book, designed to give us insight through the revelation of Jesus.

> Let us be glad and rejoice and give Him glory, for the marriage of the Lamb has come, and His wife has made herself ready. And to her it was granted to be arrayed in fine linen, clean and bright, for the fine linen is the righteous acts of the saints.
> Revelation 19:7-8

This passage reveals the bride exercising will and responsibility in the preparation process. She is not able to be passive. She must be proactive — even passionately proactive — in the preparation. The bride has made herself ready.

> Then I, John, saw the holy city, the new
> Jerusalem, coming down out of heaven from
> God, prepared as a bride beautifully dressed for
> her husband.
>
> Revelation 21:2

In that day we will be seen; the bride will be manifest.

To Stop the Purpose of God

The enemy will stop at nothing to hinder and prevent the process of the bride being made manifest; in other words for us to become one with Him. He will use every scheme he can contrive to interfere with the process. He is dependent on the response of man's carnal nature to have any degree of effect.

Satan's plan is to interrupt and defeat the process. His attack is rooted in man's carnal nature and, because of this, we have identified the attack as the attack of Jezebel. However, his effort in the end will not be enough to stand against the will of God. Since it is the will of the Father to see the bride, it will surely happen. Sadly, not every person will realize that reality; some will be overcome.

The assignment of the Jezebel spirit is to stop the purpose of God from being realized by those He has anointed for His purpose.

CHAPTER THREE

Seedbed for Destruction

For those who live according to the flesh [1] set their minds on the things of the flesh, but those who live according to the Spirit, the things of the Spirit. For to be carnally minded is death, but to be spiritually minded is life and peace.

Romans 8:5-6

So then, those who are in the flesh cannot please God.

Romans 8:8

Our flesh (our carnal nature) is the seedbed where the Jezebel spirit plants seeds of destruction to stop the purpose of God. It has no other place to manifest itself except in our carnal nature. This scripture clearly speaks of the result of moving in the flesh (being carnally minded) as "death." Often people are caught in their carnal nature, [2] and the evidence of being caught is the result that is birthed from works of the flesh.

The Birthing

The action of birth can only come after conception. In this case conception takes place when we allow our carnal nature to rule over our spirit.

> But each one is tempted when he is drawn away by his own desires and enticed. Then, when desire has conceived, it gives birth to sin; and sin, when it is full-grown, brings forth death.
>
> James 1:14-15

The work of the Holy Spirit is to convince us "of sin, of righteousness and of judgment." He is there to give guidance in every decision. When we become born again, the Holy Spirit is faithful to make us aware that we have a choice. We can walk in the flesh or we can walk in the spirit.

Making a choice to walk in the flesh opens the door for the enemy of our soul to reap a harvest of destruction. The Jezebel spirit seeks the opportunity to influence our flesh (i.e., carnal nature) by planting seeds of destruction.

In order for us to prevent the seeds of destruction from taking root, we need to have an understanding of our carnal nature and how it functions.

Our Carnal Nature

Let us consider our created being (the whole person) according to God's plan. God has created us body, soul, and spirit. These three distinct parts make up one whole human being. The evidence of these three parts is found repeatedly in Scripture. However, we will use this passage for our consideration, since Jesus mentions all three in these verses.

> Then he said to them, "My **soul** is overwhelmed with sorrow to the point of death. Stay

here and keep watch with me." Going a little farther, he fell with his face to the ground and prayed, "My Father, if it is possible, may this cup be taken from me. Yet not as I will, but as you will." Then he returned to his disciples and found them sleeping. "Could you men not keep watch with me for one hour?" he asked Peter.

"Watch and pray so that you will not fall into temptation. The **spirit** is willing, but the **body** is weak."

Matthew 26:38-41 NIV

Considering the Original Text

A closer look at these three parts of our being will be helpful to understand our carnal nature, to see how it is key to Jezebelic activity.

It will also give a clear perspective of our carnal nature so that we are not ignorant of its potential to be used.

Soul

The word *psuche*[(3)], (psoo-khay), translated soul, is a very complicated part of our being.

The soul represents our heart, the center of our being, life and mind. It is, however, directly related to our spirit. The Greek word *psuche* is rooted in another word meaning breath, which is used in the definition of the Greek word for spirit.

Spirit

The word *pneuma*[(4)], (pnyoo'-mah), which is translated spirit, is used to identify spirit figuratively; the human spirit, the rational soul, by implication; vital principle, (seat of conscience), mental disposition, etc. It comes from a word that means breath or blast of air, or a breeze.

Body

The word *sarx*,[5], which is translated as body in this passage, is a word widely used in the New Testament to identify our fleshly body. It is also used to identify our human nature with its frailties and passions; or a human being, and as such, carnal, carnality, carnally minded, flesh or fleshly.

Body: Another Perspective

There is another passage that speaks of the body from a broader perspective than just flesh or carnal nature (sarx).

If your right eye causes you to sin, gouge it out and throw it away. It is better for you to lose one part of your body than for your whole **body** to be thrown into hell.

Matthew 5:29 NIV

The word *soma*[6], which is translated body in this passage, is the most frequently used word for body in the New Testament. It is used to express the identity of our total created being and somehow speaks of our identity, thus embracing our body, spirit, and soul.

But for the purposes of this chapter we will be looking at the word body in a more defined role as one of three parts of our created being, that of our flesh, carnal nature (*sarx*).

The Interaction of Our Created Being

The body, soul, and spirit (our created being) are interacting continually. The result of their responding to one another establishes the foundation and motivation of all our actions.

These actions and the foundation for them will be what we are recognized by, such as our personality and our character (i.e. he is an evil person... he is a good person... he is a thoughtful person... considerate, kind, slanderous, a gossip, trustworthy, lazy). All of these distinguishing characteristics make up our personality and define our character.

Each part of our being has a specific role and function in producing a whole being. For example, if the soul and spirit did not have the participation of the body, the result would not represent a whole functioning being.

The same would be true if any part of our being was not participating in the whole. This is why God does not deliver our carnal nature from us (our body, our created being, as a whole *soma*); without it we are not able to represent a total human being.

In order for us to understand further the complicated make up of God's created man, we need to consider how the three parts relate to one another, each part making a contribution of its own value to make up the whole.

The Spirit's Effect on the Soul
The soul is the heart of man. It is the center of our being, life, and mind.

> The LORD saw how great man's wickedness on the earth had become, and that every inclination of the thoughts of his heart was only evil all the time.
> Genesis 6:5 NIV

> The good man brings good things out of the good stored up in his heart, and the evil man brings evil things out of the evil stored up in his heart. For out of the overflow of his heart his mouth speaks.
> Luke 6:45 NIV

The soul is interrelated with the body and the spirit of man. Both the spirit and the body impact the soul, resulting in an action of the heart.

The Spirit Establishes Conscience Awareness

The spirit impacts the soul with conscience awareness and mental disposition.

It is the spirit that establishes the seat of conscience awareness in our being. This is the place where we establish conscience standards that dictate to our soul a principled value standard that challenges or releases certain actions that would be otherwise unchecked. The result of violating our conscience is guilt. Guilt is an emotion that is resident in our soul, initiated by the conscience standard imposed by our spirit. This emotion of guilt at times limits our actions and at other times requires us to make an effort to right a wrong action.

The Spirit Establishes Mental Disposition

The spirit brings to the soul our mental disposition. Disposition is defined as "a putting in order or being put in order," in other words, one's customary frame of mind, nature, or temperament.

For example, when we are responding to something with peace in our heart, that peace is the evidence of our disposition. The peace flowing out of our spirit brings stability to the heart, the center of our being, our soul.

When I think of this reality, the great hymn "It Is Well With My Soul" comes to mind. The writer of the hymn (Horatio G. Spafford) experienced the loss of five children in the space of one year, first his son in a fire and then four daughters at sea. He was devastated by this great loss and suffered unbearable anguish, yet his mental disposition expresses, "it is well with my soul."

The Flesh's (carnal nature's) Effect on the Soul

The flesh (our carnal nature, carnality, being carnally-minded, flesh or fleshly desires) impacts the soul with its frailties and passions. The influence of our carnal nature, being rooted in the flesh, can have a devastating effect on our total being if it is in control.

If left to itself, our flesh (carnal nature) will even consume itself with its evil desires. Basically this means that when our flesh is left completely to itself, it will self-destruct.

The Soul's Effect on the Flesh

The soul impacts the flesh with emotion, desire, lust, passion, intellect, and conscience awareness that comes from the spirit. This impact can be positive or negative, depending on the response of the soul to the spirit and flesh of man.

Our actions are the result of our soul (emotions, desires, and thought processes) dictating to our flesh (carnal nature) the course of action that will take place.

They seem to impregnate and cooperate with one another. The inherent weakness here in this unique relationship seems to be driven by mutual gratification. The actions of our being are a result of this impregnation and cooperation, which takes place between these two elements. There is no action unless the flesh is drawn into the expressed desires of the soul.

> Let no one say when he is tempted, "I am tempted by God"; for God cannot be tempted by evil, nor does He Himself tempt anyone. But each one is tempted when he is drawn away by his own desires and enticed. Then, when desire has conceived, it gives birth to sin; and sin, when it is full-grown, brings forth death.
>
> James 1:13-15

If left to themselves, these two elements of our created being are destined for moral and ethical failure.

The Spirit's Effect on the Flesh and the Soul
It is extremely important to understand the dynamics of the relationship of the spirit to the soul and the flesh. When we grasp the dynamics of the spirit in relationship to the soul and the flesh, we will see how God's design of our created being and the presence of the Holy Spirit is all we need to live a victorious life.

This aspect of our being, the spirit of man (rational soul), by implication; vital principle, (our seat of conscience), mental disposition etc., is crucial in God's design. It is the place God has designed in us to receive Him, the place where He becomes Lord through Jesus, the Christ. The spirit has the potential to ultimately influence the soul and body to bring about godly character and victorious living as we grow in the likeness of Christ.

Why do we find the spirit of man is the place where God chooses to dwell and communicate with him? To answer this question, I ask you to consider a passage found in Job.

But it is the spirit in a man, the breath of the Almighty, that gives him understanding.
Job 32:8 NIV

Perhaps from God's perspective, by implication, it is the spirit of man (the breath of the Almighty) that is the only aspect of our created being He can trust.

A New Standard for Expressing Our lives
The spirit of man lacks the benefit of the presence of God and His kingdom until he is born again (born of the Spirit, born from above). At that point God brings to our spirit a righteous standard that was not there before.

Before we are born again we have a conscience standard, but it is based on our knowledge and experience from an earthly realm. When we have the presence of the Holy Spirit, the foundation for our conscience standard changes from our knowledge and experience from an earthly realm to a standard of righteousness from a heavenly realm. That heavenly realm is His kingdom.

> But about the Son he says, "Your throne, O God, will last for ever and ever, and righteousness will be the scepter of your kingdom."
> Hebrews 1:8

The kingdom of God is ruled by a scepter of righteousness. That is His standard. God's desire is for this same standard of righteousness to reign and rule in our hearts.

If the kingdom of God is to rule in our hearts, then our soul needs to yield to the righteous standard that has taken up residence within us, and that happens through the relational dynamics between the soul and the spirit of man.

Flesh and Spirit Are Contrary

One thing we want to remember is that the spirit and the flesh are contrary to one another[7]. Since this is the case, the only way the spirit can influence the flesh is through the soul.

Even though the spirit has established a seat of moral conscience, the flesh still wants to follow its desires. It is the soul of man that dictates to the flesh the activity that happens as a result of the influence of the spirit.

The flesh has a tendency to rebel against the spirit, and it does so effectively. This happens by the flesh raising the heat of its passions, lusts, and desires to the point where it convinces the soul (with this heightened intensity) that its inclination must be the right thing to do.

However, it cannot move forward with an action unless the soul cooperates. If the cooperation of the soul requires it to violate the conscience standard of the spirit, the result will be guilt. If the conscience standard that is being violated is the righteous standard that Jesus brings, then the result is not only guilt, but sin as well.

Free Will
The will of man is seated in his soul. The soul's liberty to choose to compromise or not to compromise its values is called free will. How we choose to exercise our will is determined by the influence coming from our spirit and our flesh (our carnal nature). There is a tendency for the soul to compromise the righteous standard that is in place, due to the influence of the flesh. This tendency to compromise comes because the soul and flesh (carnal nature) are driven by mutual gratification.

Dying to Self

The first time I heard this term I was not sure what it meant. I've come to understand that Jesus gave us an example to follow, and the example demonstrates to us how we should live. The Scriptures are clear about this example.

When he had finished washing their feet, he put on his clothes and returned to his place. "Do you understand what I have done for you?" he asked them. "You call me 'Teacher' and 'Lord', and rightly so, for that is what I am. Now that I, your Lord and Teacher, have washed your feet, you also should wash one another's feet. I have set you an example that you should do as I have done for you. I tell you the truth, no servant is greater than his master, nor is a messenger greater than the one who sent him."

John 13:12-16 NIV

In this passage we see Jesus laying aside His rightful place as Lord (dying to self) and taking on the role of a servant. Dying to self basically means giving up your position.

In our case, and for the purpose of this chapter, the definition of "our position" is: what we think; our perspective; that which is the driving force of our actions. We need to die to self and put to death the deeds of the flesh (carnal nature).

Put to death, therefore, whatever belongs to your earthly nature: sexual immorality, impurity, lust, evil desires and greed, which is idolatry.

Colossians 3:5 NIV

The Spirit of Man Embraces Its Destiny

God has placed within every human being a spirit, and the destiny of that spirit can only be realized by spiritual new birth: believing in God through His Son Jesus, thus inheriting eternal life. It is up to us to embrace the destiny we have in Him.

We not only have a destiny, but we also have the promise of victorious life here on earth.

For Christ died for sins once for all, the righteous for the unrighteous, to bring you to God. He was put to death in the body but made alive by the Spirit,

1 Peter 3:18 NIV

Therefore, if anyone is in Christ, he is a new creation; the old has gone, the new has come!

2 Corinthians 5:17 NIV

Refusing to Embrace His Destiny

I sat across from a young brother who had put himself in such a hard place by his own ambition, and my heart was filled with grief. He had such potential, but all that God desired for him was now at risk because of some actions he took based on what he perceived as an injustice done toward him.

"Pastor, it's your fault that I have not been able to realize the call God has on my life. It is obvious to everyone except you that I have an exceptional gift of teaching. You leave me no other recourse; I've made a decision, and I am going to start my own Bible study.

You should also know there are several others in the church who feel you have lost the anointing to lead this church. They will be joining me until we can determine what God has in mind. We have met several times and believe that God might be calling us out to start a new church."

Not Dying to Self

This brother had taken a position of not dying to self and had left the door open for his flesh to be out of control.

If you have any encouragement from being united with Christ, if any comfort from his love, if any fellowship with the Spirit, if any tenderness and compassion, then make my joy complete by being like-minded, having the same love, being one in spirit and purpose. Do nothing out of selfish ambition or vain conceit, but in humility consider others better than yourselves. Each of you should look not only to your own interests, but also to the interests of others. Your attitude should be the same as that of Christ Jesus.

Philippians 2:1-5 NIV

My young brother was moving out of selfish ambition; his whole perspective was from a place of self-centeredness. **After he conceived something from the desire in his heart, he exercised his influence to affect others. (This is a perfect example of Jezebelic activity in the church.)**

Dying to Self

When we attend to the interest of others and are not focused on ourselves, God is able to move us to our highest potential. When we are self-centered, we have already reached our highest potential.

> This I say, therefore, and testify in the Lord, that you should no longer walk as the rest of the Gentiles walk, in the futility of their mind, having their understanding darkened, being alienated from the life of God, because of the ignorance that is in them, because of the blindness of their heart; who, being past feeling, have given themselves over to lewdness, to work all uncleanness with greediness. But you have not so learned Christ,
>
> Ephesians 4:17-20

The Scriptures speak to us extensively about the need to die to self and instead walk in a manner pleasing to God. Paul's exhortation to no longer live as the Gentiles do is consistent throughout his writing.

We will not know the victory we have until we know the power that has been released in our lives through our death to self.

CHAPTER FOUR

Modus Operandi of the Jezebel Spirit

> I urge you, brothers, to watch out for those who cause divisions and put obstacles in your way that are contrary to the teaching you have learned. Keep away from them. For such people are not serving our Lord Christ, but their own appetites. By smooth talk and flattery they deceive the minds of naive people.
>
> Romans 16:17-18 NIV

Webster's Dictionary defines modus operandi (m.o.) as a term used to describe a way of doing or accomplishing something. I want again to quote Dutch Sheets,[1] "If you don't know what you're looking for, you probably won't find it." We need all the help we can get in order to identify the attack of the Jezebel spirit. In this chapter I want to identify some of the key characteristics of the m.o. of a Jezebelic attack.

There Is Nothing Worse Than Being "Blindsided"
That is, to get hit without the benefit of knowing it's

coming. When I played football in high school, I discovered very quickly that getting blind-sided was devastating because you are not prepared for it. The vulnerability and surprise catches you totally defenseless.

My first experience at being blind-sided was during a play called a "trap play." The play was setup so there was an open hole in the offensive line. This allowed the defensive player to easily go through the hole.

I remember it as though it were yesterday. I was a freshman, excited about playing high school football, and I really wanted to impress the coach. I had been in for several plays as a defensive linebacker, looking eagerly for a chance to sack the quarterback.

The ball was snapped and there it was: a wide-open hole in the offensive line. I charged through the line with my eye on the quarterback and wham! I was introduced to being "blind-sided."

I found myself on my back gasping for breath and trying to focus my eyes. My ears were ringing and I was sure that I wouldn't be able to stand on my own. Just then, Harry, a senior and the first-string guard, stuck out his hand to help me up and said past a big grin, "Caught ya nappin."

Being Blindsided by Jezebelic Activity

That is all too often the case when it comes to the attack of the Jezebel spirit. We find ourselves getting sucked into the trap only to be "caught nappin." In this chapter we will be taking a closer look at the modus operandi of the Jezebel spirit. The more we learn and understand the m.o., the more effectively we will overcome the attack.

By the way, it took getting hit a few more times before I began to recognize the signs of the "Trap Play" as it developed. I'm praying that this book will help you recognize the signs of the Jezebelic "Trap Play."

Job Description of the Jezebel Spirit

The following passage of scripture gives revelation about the activity of the Jezebel spirit. While studying the book of Revelation, I noticed a verse that seems to reveal what the job description of the Jezebel spirit is, if indeed it has one. It is a passage describing Satan's activity.

> He opened his mouth to blaspheme[2] God, and to slander[3] his name and his dwelling place and those who live in heaven.
> Revelation 13:6 NIV

Not only is he blaspheming God, he is also slandering His dwelling place. This speaks of the attack, not only against God, but also against us, because we are His dwelling place.

The Malignancy

What does it mean to blaspheme God and to slander His name and His dwelling place? "Blasphemy" is practically confined to speech that is defamatory of God's divine majesty. Defamatory means to defame. To defame means: to attack or injure the reputation or honor of by false and malicious statements, to malign, slander or libel, malign to plot, deceive, wicked, malicious, to speak evil of, showing ill will, malicious, very harmful, **malignant**[4].·

It is interesting to note that blasphemy is defamatory speech that has roots tying it to malignancy. We know how wicked and destructive a malignancy is to the physical body. A malignancy in the spiritual body is just as deadly unless it is dealt with. This book is about recognizing, confronting, and overcoming the Jezebelic attack, which is like a malignancy in the local church, with all its potential horror.

The Assignment of the Jezebel Spirit

Chapter Two is devoted in depth to the assignment of the Jezebel spirit. However, in brief, its assignment is to defeat the vision and plan of God by causing God's anointed to be dysfunctional, to destroy God's anointed, and to stop the voice of God in the earth.

Wrapped in the Carnal Nature

It is important to recognize that the attack of the Jezebel spirit is uniquely wrapped in the carnal nature of man. There are other kinds of attacks initiated by Satan against the church that are not spawned and birthed out of the carnal nature of man. These attacks are no less devastating and need to be addressed. They are also subject to the authority that is resident within us.

> And Jesus came and spoke to them, saying, "All authority has been given to Me in heaven and on earth."
>
> Matthew 28:18

However, from a tactical standpoint, the spiritual warfare against the attack of the Jezebel spirit is uniquely different, because you are dealing with man's carnal nature. When you are dealing with demonic activity resulting in oppression or affliction, you can cast it out by the grace and power of God. But when you are dealing with man's carnal nature, you cannot cast it out. There will be more discussion about this in Chapter Fifteen.

We Have Been Empowered

The focus of the attack of a Jezebelic spirit is against those whom God has anointed for His purpose, and it is relentless in its attack.

Now it is God who makes both us and you stand firm in Christ. He anointed us, set his seal of ownership on us, and put his Spirit in our hearts as a deposit, guaranteeing what is to come.

2 Corinthians 1:21-22 NIV

We have been empowered to stand firm in His calling on our lives: that we are men and women redeemed by the blood of the Lamb to be the fullness of Him in the face of the earth. The church exists by the sovereign will of God and with predetermined purpose. Not only is the church the bride, but it is God's voice in the earth as well as His instrument for exercising judgment against Satan.

The Objective of the Attack

The objective of the Jezebelic attack is to cause the church to be dysfunctional, thus destroying the purpose of God. The focus of the attack is against the anointed of God who are set in place to accomplish His good and perfect will.

We Have a Guarantee

In light of the fact that we are under attack continuously from the enemy of our soul, I want to bring our focus to another fact. The first time I saw the book "The Bride Wore Combat Boots,"[5] which was written by our friend, Dotty Schmitt, I was very intrigued by the title. I want you to know that not only does she wear combat boots; she also has everything she needs to win the battle. We have been anointed to stand firm and be victorious. We must understand this about the enemy of our soul: he is relentless in his attack. Yet, our guarantee is total victory in Christ Jesus!

The Operative Word Is Influence

The Jezebel spirit has a clearly identifiable strategy to accomplish its goal, to prevent the church from reaching her divine destiny that was determined by God from the beginning of creation.

Influence Impacts Others

There is a specific element that must be a part of the equation of the Jezebelic attack. That specific element is **influence**. I would even say it is the **operative word** when it comes to the effectiveness of the attack. There are other elements that will be involved in the attack that find their roots in our carnal nature. However, none of these elements will accomplish the devastation intended if there is no influence. The Jezebel spirit is looking for opportunities in places where there is influence to see its assignment fulfilled.

In Chapter Two I wrote about Satan's attack against God's purposes in the Garden of Eden. Satan chose to approach Eve in his attack. I have heard some say that the reason he approached Eve was due to the fact that she was the weaker vessel. The truth is, both vessels were weak in the flesh when it came to standing against the attack of Satan.

> It was granted to him to make war with the saints and to overcome them. And authority was given him over every tribe, tongue, and nation. All who dwell on the earth will worship him, whose names have not been written in the Book of Life of the Lamb slain from the foundation of the world.
>
> Revelation 13:7-8

Why did he approach Eve first? May I suggest it was because she was the stronger vessel when it came to influence. God has graced women with the gift of influence. Every man knows the truth of this and I am sure women do also, to a great extent. If Satan had approached Adam first, the chance of Adam influencing Eve in the same way that she influenced him was slim.

Please don't misunderstand; **I'm talking about influence, not gender.** Too often the Jezebel spirit is genderized as female. That is a great mistake and serves to bring confusion to the identity of Jezebelic activity.

The Jezebel Spirit Uses People of Influence

This is a great truth that gives us insight into the working of a Jezebelic spirit in our midst. This spirit is looking for people of influence to accomplish its goal. Someone who comes to the Lord on Sunday morning does not split the church on Wednesday. Why? Because they aren't in a position of influence to be used in that way.

The Jezebel spirit has its best opportunity for devastation when it works through someone who's in a position of influence and whose flesh is out of control. This combination guarantees success in the attack. The "seed-bed" is ready for seeds of destruction. (See Chapter Three.)

We Are All in the Same Place

Everyone has a degree of influence and a carnal nature. Based on these facts, we must acknowledge that everyone has the potential to be used by the Jezebel spirit.

There are some who believe their capacity to sin does not exist in the new creature they are in Christ. Do not be deceived; we all have a carnal nature. God does not remove our carnal nature from us, but He does deliver us **from** our carnal nature. The fallacy is for any individual to feel they are beyond the potential use of the Jezebel spirit.

People of Influence in the Church

Where do we find people of influence in the local church? The most obvious place is in positions of leadership. However, there are others who have established a sphere of influence by virtue of personality, ability, education, relationship, or status. Many times people of influence are found in the pews, a place of seeming anonymity.

Focused Attack

People who are serving in an area of ministry need to be especially guarded. They are targeted and used in Jezebelic activity because of their position of influence. Jezebelic activity needs influence to launch an effective attack against a ministry.

The objective of the attack is to bring the ministry to a place of being dysfunctional. This dysfunctionality will then cause the church and her leaders to constantly be in recovery mode, wasting precious time, energy, and resources that should be used to fulfill its God-ordained mission. A church depleted of time, energy and resources will never reach God's intended purpose. We must stay on course and stop the attack of the Jezebel spirit.

Without influence, the Jezebel spirit has no foundation for launching its attack against the purposes of God.

Obvious People of Influence

Here is a list of people who have the greatest influence in the church. Remember, everyone has some degree of influence. We each become a potential hazard when we exercise our influence in the flesh.

Many times the strategy of the enemy is to use leaders who are functioning as apostles, prophets, teachers, evangelists, pastors, elders, worship leaders, intercessors, and deacons. Satan is also more than willing to use any other ministry leaders as well as the saints.

Jezebelic activity, whatever its ploy, is not limited to leadership. We are all vulnerable to being used in Jezebelic activity since we all have a carnal nature and some degree of influence.

In part two of this book, we will look at several areas of ministry that frequently come under the pressure of Jezebelic activity. Even if you serve in an area of ministry not mentioned, you are still vulnerable to this attack. The point is, we all are to walk circumspectly when we are relating to one another on different levels of influence, whether we are being influenced or are the ones in a position of influencing others.

The Jezebelic Spirit Is Relentless

We had just come through a most painful experience. I wondered at times if we would survive. It seemed like it would never end. It was like being in the midst of a hurricane. Do you know what it is like being in a hurricane? Everything is out of control and the only hope is to hang on until it passes.

The destruction was unbelievable; I never thought I would see anything like this in the church. The name of the "hurricane" was Myra, the head of our intercessory prayer ministry. The hurricane had passed over us, and now it was cleanup time.

People were constantly trying to encourage me, saying things such as, "The attack is over. This one or that one has left the church; you know, the one who was causing all the strife and contention. It is like a breath of fresh air, now that the problem has been solved."

Reader, this is just so far from the truth. The truth is, the Jezebelic attack is never over; it just quietly awaits a new face, looking for someone whose flesh has risen up out of control, to become a seedbed for the next offensive. Each of us must be on guard or we can get "caught nappin" and become a vehicle of destruction for the enemy. (See Chapter Nine, "Stopping the Jezebelic Attack.")

Jezebelic Strategy

The word "credibility" means to be believable, trustworthy, and reliable. If someone's credibility is destroyed, a cloud of doubt has imprisoned all that they are. They no longer have the liberty to freely serve the Lord. It doesn't matter whether the issues that destroyed the credibility are true or not, because the result is the same: credibility is destroyed or impeded for a season. Since this is such a vital area, it becomes the key tactic of the attack of the Jezebel spirit.

1. Credibility Relies on Integrity

When I was in Bible school, I remember hearing of a situation that developed in a pastor's office. I'm not sure if the story is true, but it does serve well to make this point.

A woman came into the church office requesting to see the pastor. The secretary, who was at her desk, showed the woman through her office and into the pastor's office. She closed his door and the woman sat across the desk from him. After chatting for a few minutes about the weather and other insignificant things, something happened that devastated the pastor, his family, and his ministry. The woman suddenly stood, screamed, and ripped open her blouse. The pastor, in shock, ran to her aid and was standing by her side when the secretary burst through the door in response to her screams. "He attacked me, he attacked me," the woman yelled.

In a split second his integrity was in question and his credibility was put in jeopardy. Was it true? ... Was it fair? ... The answer is no, but the result was the same. Now the question is, how likely is it that this would happen? I'm sure this pastor had never considered it.

This spirit seeks to destroy credibility by destroying integrity. Integrity means to be steadfast; adhering to a strict moral or ethical code; soundness; completeness. Integrity can quickly and easily be destroyed with a few words. In my years as a pastor I found that my integrity was precious and needed to be guarded.

When integrity is destroyed, so is credibility, and once that happens, credibility is extremely hard to rebuild and perhaps may never be totally restored. Credibility is destroyed because integrity is directly related to trust; it is impossible to trust someone who has no integrity. When the trust factor is gone, effectual ministry is gone also.

It takes only a word to begin to cast doubt and bring integrity into question. "Did you hear" or "are you aware" often begin a sentence that will contain words that damage or destroy integrity. The Jezebel spirit uses the tongue that is rooted in the flesh to set fire to one's integrity.

2. The Foundation of Integrity Is Character

Integrity is dependent on a foundation of character. Often the enemy is seeking to destroy character because he knows it is crucial to the trust level that is established in relationships. If a man's character is brought into question, immediately his reputation is at stake. Reputation is what we are known by. The reasoning follows that if someone's character is flawed, then integrity must be lacking also, and so therefore they have no credibility.

The Jezebel spirit's m.o. is to bring into question the character of the one who is the focus of the attack.

> Jezebel his wife said, "Is this how you act as king over Israel? Get up and eat! Cheer up. I'll get you the vineyard of Naboth the Jezreelite." So she wrote letters in Ahab's name, placed his seal on them, and sent them to the elders and

nobles who lived in Naboth's city with him. In those letters she wrote: "Proclaim a day of fasting and seat Naboth in a prominent place among the people. But seat two scoundrels opposite him and have them testify that he has cursed both God and the king. Then take him out and stone him to death."

1 Kings 21:7-10

Remember the job description of the Jezebel spirit we talked about earlier — that of blaspheming God and His dwelling place? The woman, Jezebel, did exactly that; she destroyed Naboth's character and his integrity with words.

Since good character is the foundation of our integrity, we can reason that if our character is tarnished, the resulting loss of integrity will bring into question our credibility. With our credibility in question, effective ministry is diminished. Using the vehicle of flesh out of control, the Jezebelic spirit will begin to attack the personal character of God's anointed minister through malicious gossip, lies, half-truths, deception, and misrepresentation. Why is it that most people, when exposed to gossip, are easily drawn into the character demolition process?

3. The Jezebel Spirit Seeks to Destroy Unity

The Scriptures are very clear about the significance of unity. We see many areas where the Scripture sets unity high on the list of desirable attributes in the body of Christ.

I would draw our attention to two scriptures in particular. The first is found in Ephesians chapter four. Because of the context of this scripture, we recognize it as part of the foundation for the introduction of the ministry gifts to the church[6].

> Make every effort to keep the unity of the Spirit through the bond of peace.
>
> Ephesians 4:3 NIV

Unity is not only a part of the foundation for the introduction of the ministry gifts to the church, but it is also key and essential in order for the ministry gifts to be received.

Why is this a crucial area for the Jezebel spirit to attack? The ministry gifts are set in place by Jesus to bring maturity so that we may attain the whole measure of the fullness of Christ[7]. I can assure you that the enemy of our soul does not want the church to mature and grow into the whole measure of the fullness of Christ.

He will do everything he can to destroy unity in the church, which when effectively destroyed also destroys the integrity of the foundation (which is the first step to becoming mature, that is, attaining to the whole measure of the fullness of Christ).

The second passage is found in the book of Psalms and is often quoted in a gathering of churches and leaders. When it is quoted, a sense of well-being floods over the assembly.

> Behold, how good and how pleasant it is for brethren to dwell together in unity! It is like the precious oil upon the head, Running down on the beard, the beard of Aaron, Running down on the edge of his garments. It is like the dew of Hermon, Descending upon the mountains of Zion; for there the LORD commanded the blessing — Life forevermore
>
> Psalm 133:1-3

What a tremendous passage, full of great promise. God initiates an action; He commands a blessing because of the unity. In the NIV translation it says He bestows a blessing.

These are strong words, bestow and command, and they are translated from a word in the original text that means to constitute[8]. Let's think about this for a moment: God exercises His will to constitute His blessing because of unity. I believe He continues to bestow and command a blessing when He sees brethren dwelling together in unity.

So this is what we've learned: that unity is an active word that requires our participation and is essential to the foundation for becoming mature, attaining to the whole measure of the fullness of Christ. We also learned that unity brings about the blessing of God. The enemy of our soul does not want us to have either.

Think about your church home and how many times and in what variety of ways the unity of the congregation is challenged. The destruction of unity starts with one person and is then spread by influence to others. When we see this happening in the church, it is most likely an attack of the Jezebel spirit.

4. The Issue Is Control

The Jezebel spirit wants control and seeks to have it. Control determines direction and outcome. There are four methods the Jezebel spirit uses to take control.

a. Intimidation Has One Goal: To Dominate

The first is intimidation; you have seen this one in action, I'm sure. As a pastor I have had people approach me with a need to validate what they are about to say. So the conversation usually goes this way: "I have just finished a forty-day fast. During the fast I read eight books on prayer by the current most significant authors writing on prayer. God gave me six revelations about personal prayer and prayer in the church. I would like to meet with you today for lunch to discuss what is on my heart about the direction for prayer in the church." The truth is, I, the pastor, haven't done any of those things in the past forty days, and this increases my propensity toward being intimidated!

To be fair, this approach isn't always Jezebelic activity. Sometimes it is just someone wanting to express something and struggling with their insecurity. (this aggressive action is still a flesh or carnal nature issue and unacceptable). However, I have often seen Jezebelic influence in this type of situation. It will establish an environment of intimidation in order to take control. Remember, control determines direction and outcome. The assignment of the Jezebel spirit is to stop the purposes of God. Intimidation gives a foothold for the Jezebel spirit to determine the outcome.

b. Domination Is Often Used to Gain Submission

The second area is domination. Webster's dictionary defines domination as: 1: supremacy or preeminence over another; 2: exercise of mastery, ruling power, or preponderant influence.

When we become subject to domination, which is to submit to whatever force is being applied, we are no longer in control of our destiny. When someone is overwhelmed by intimidation, they become very vulnerable to domination. Domination has its effect by a demonstration of superiority. It will claim superiority in significant areas that produce leadership capabilities (i.e., "I have read eight books," and "God gave me six revelations.") What this spirit is saying through the other person is, "I am the one most qualified."

Domination is often a partner to intimidation, but not always. There are times when we are dominated as a result of our own apathy. We can become overwhelmed and suffer burnout through sheer emotional exhaustion and fatigue or a loss of passion, resulting in apathy. For the Jezebel spirit, the issue is control. If the Jezebel spirit can find people who have become apathetic, taking control of them through domination becomes less difficult.

c. Manipulation Is the Base Activity of Witchcraft

The third is manipulation. Intimidation and domination are the front-runners for manipulation. Manipulation is the operative word for control. Webster's dictionary gives this definition; to influence especially with intent to deceive. Manipulation as it pertains to Jezebelic activity is simply one individual being controlled by another to accomplish selfish goals and ambitions.

Sometimes we see people manipulating one another in an effort to get their own way. Manipulation is clearly rooted in the carnal nature. The Jezebel spirit seeks to use someone who is good at manipulation to accomplish Satan's objective, that is, to stop the purposes of God. Again, the issue is control. However, the reality of being controlled by the specific objectives of another person cannot be realized without manipulation.

Intimidation and domination set up the individual to be manipulated. The objective is for the Jezebelic spirit to have control. The one who is in control determines the outcome.

d. Seduction: Another Approach

The fourth is seduction. Seduction stands alone as a basic tactic to gain control. The reason it stands alone is because it is totally unrelated to intimidation and domination. Intimidation and domination produce an emotional trauma that causes the individual to be vulnerable to manipulation.

Seduction has a very different effect. It appeals to the emotions and the flesh in such a way that the individual being seduced becomes intoxicated. That is, they are not able to respond to the situation with soundness of thought and action. The seduction can be intellectual, emotional, physical, or a combination of all three, appealing to the senses of the flesh (carnal nature).

The Jezebel spirit often uses sexuality to break down the defenses of an individual. (Often when addressing this area people use the word sex rather than sexuality). I have chosen the word sexuality instead of the word sex, because the word sex primarily refers to gender or a sexual act. The word sexuality refers to sexual character or potency. Sexuality, when used as a tool for seduction, has a strong pull on the emotions, the intellect, and the physical body. When any combination of these is overwhelmed by the character and potency of sexuality, the result is seduction. Keep in mind that we are all subject to the ploy of seduction simply because we have a carnal nature that seeks satisfaction. But, this seductive ploy becomes a reality if and when it takes the position of controlling our destiny through our carnal nature.

Not All Seduction Is Sexual

The face of seduction is not always sexual. I know leaders who guard themselves diligently when it comes to sexual issues, yet completely let down their guard in other areas where they can be seduced. Seduction can take the form of anything that might be used to gain favor by satisfying the flesh. Gifts, compliments, and flattery given as a vehicle to win favor are all tools of seduction. It isn't only leaders who fall prey to this ploy. Be on guard!

An individual can become so intoxicated by seduction that he or she will do irresponsible things. This intoxication causes the individual to become vulnerable to manipulation. Again, the issue is control. The Jezebel spirit will not stop trying to gain control. Control determines the outcome.

5. Confusion Is the Hallmark of the Jezebelic Attack

The Jezebel spirit seeks to establish the environment in which an attack can be the most fruitful. While watching a documentary on World War II, I was intrigued by the amount of time and effort spent in creating the right environment for the U.S. forces to be successful in their battles. In particular, I watched a naval battle unfolding. Since the battle was on the high seas there were no mountains or trees to hide behind. They sent a ship up and down the battle line with thick billowing clouds of manufactured smoke to hide behind as they launched their attack.

The Jezebel spirit uses the same strategy to launch its attack. It is never a straight-on confrontation; the attack is always clothed in confusion. Confusion is a smoke screen that distorts reality. The word confusion means to be unclear in mind or purpose. If someone can keep you in a state of confusion, you will not respond well to the situation.

Confusion establishes the most advantageous environment for the manipulation and control by the Jezebel spirit. If you don't know where the attack is coming from, it will be hard to defeat. You will use tremendous amounts of energy and resources to try to stand against the attack, but until the confusion is dealt with, your efforts will not be successful.

We need to recognize our inability to take clear decisive action in a state of confusion. Following are four ways the Jezebel spirit establishes an environment of confusion that serves as a smoke screen from which to launch its attack.

The Jezebel Spirit Uses Lies

The first is lying. A lie is a false statement deliberately presented as true. We need to remember that Satan is the father of lies. The Jezebel spirit will use a blatant lie to achieve its objectives, to establish a smoke screen, to create a state of confusion. When decisions are made based on a lie, we give place for the destruction that will come as a consequence of that lie. When our foundation is a lie, then reality becomes a phantom. **A lie holds people in bondage as long as the lie is believed**. It is the truth that sets man free.

The Jezebel Spirit Uses Deception

The second is deception. We need to understand the difference between lying and being deceitful. A lie is more deliberate and open, where deception is more covert. Being deceitful is misrepresenting something or someone to another, leading him or her astray. Sometimes people are led astray without a word being spoken; simply withholding information is enough to lead someone astray. **Intentionally allowing someone to have a wrong impression is deception in its purist form.** When we have been deceived and begin to address issues from a foundation flawed by that deception, our responses will be faulty.

Deceitful people are cunning and do not want to be held accountable for their involvement. They maintain anonymity and a posture of innocence. It is hard to effectively call to account someone who does not seem directly responsible. In many cases people who are responsible, as deceivers are never exposed. They just allow it to happen and if someone else is blamed, they live to deceive someone else, another day. This is why the Jezebelic spirit seeks out people who are prone to deception: this tactic is an ideal smoke screen, it establishes confusion, and it's the perfect environment from which to launch an attack.

The Jezebel Spirit Uses Criticism

The third is criticism. Criticism, when used by the Jezebel sprit, is destructive beyond belief. There are some people who are known for their critical nature. The word critical is defined as "being inclined to judge severely." Criticism is the act of judging.

Overwhelmed by a Critical Spirit

The sunlight streaming through the window at the diner seemed to illuminate the steam escaping from the coffee. Swirling lazily from the cup, the steam served as an invitation to wrap my hands around the warm mug.

I used to look forward to my morning meetings with Tim, but this was going to be a hard day. I never thought I would be announcing an end to our frequent times of fellowship over coffee. I just couldn't do it any more. I always try to maintain a good attitude toward the leadership of the church, but it seems that after meeting with Tim, I usually go away feeling weighed down and defeated. Our time together is one layer of criticism on another.

The truth is, nobody is perfect, and everyone can be criticized about something. Even Tim recognizes that our times together are not edifying. He just blows it off by saying he has a critical nature. I thought I was strong enough to listen without it affecting my perspective, but after I listen to him, my confidence is shaken in the leadership and the vision of the church.

I really can't do this anymore. I wonder why he stays in the church when he sees so many things that are wrong from his perspective. God help me to speak clearly my desire, for conversation that is life-giving, strengthening, and encouraging. Here he comes now ...

Mislabeled Criticism

The Jezebel spirit is looking to use people who will covertly destroy confidence in the leadership and the vision of the church. People who are prone to be critical will do exactly that. Many times they are deceived and do not see how they are being used to accomplish the objective of the Jezebelic spirit. They will justify their actions by saying it's just their nature to be critical. They will further legitimize their action by saying they are even critical of themselves, as though it were a license to be critical of others.

This critical activity is very hard to identify because it is sometimes mislabeled as constructive criticism. Constructive criticism seeks to strengthen and encourage by being shared with the right people at the right time, to make a difference. Criticism that is launched with no particular motive other than "it is my nature to be critical" is uniquely damaging not only to those who are being criticized, but also to those who listen. The Jezebel spirit, desiring to use flesh that is out of control, is looking for just this kind of opportunity to accomplish its objective. A critical nature is not a fruit of the Spirit; it is a fruit of the flesh.

Many times those with a critical nature are never exposed because they are skillful at expressing themselves without being caught. This clandestine activity gives birth to confusion and is an effective smoke screen from which to launch an attack. Be careful when this critical nature is exposed and challenged; it can become volatile.

The Jezebel Spirit Uses Surprise

The fourth is surprise. The element of surprise is advantageous when engaging in warfare. The surprise attacker always causes confusion in its prey, because the attack comes suddenly, without warning or anticipation.

Responding Poorly

It was my thirtieth birthday and Lois wanted us to go to the family cottage at the lake. It was unseasonably warm for the 10th of May. I'd had a very busy day at the office and was embracing her idea for an evening at the lake with great joy.

As we approached the cottage, which belongs to my father and mother-in-law, I was shocked to see people on the front lawn. It was early in the season and the cottage hadn't been opened yet. As we approached the cottage, I realized the people I saw were our friends. *How incredulous*, I thought angrily, *the audacity of our friends, to come and use my in-laws' cottage without permission!* I struggled to get control of my emotions; my response to my friends was cold and disbelieving. I found it next to impossible to be cordial.

It was ten or fifteen minutes before my wife guided me over to the table to see — you guessed it — a birthday cake with "Happy Birthday Don" on it. I was totally surprised, shocked, and confused. By the way, I loved it once I got the picture.

A lot of people don't like surprise birthday parties or surprise anything else. I think that response is directly related to feeling vulnerable and out of control. When it comes to warfare that is the whole point of using the element of surprise.

Paralyzed With Disbelief

As the people of the administrative council walked through the door, my heart was filled with joy. I had been away for two weeks and, as in the past, when I draw away from the daily activities of the church I get a renewed sense of vision and direction. I was eager for this meeting, eager to share the new things on my heart with the leadership. I couldn't wait to begin the process that would bring fresh revelation and encouragement to this congregation that God has called me to pastor.

I didn't notice at first, as they gathered around the table, but soon it was obvious by their glances toward one another that they knew something I did not. As we opened with prayer God brought a peace to my heart, and an anointing of grace was evident within my heart. Before our meeting could begin, Harry, the one where all the glances seemed to be directed, spoke. "Pastor, while you were gone we met together to discuss the needs of the church. As a result of our meeting, we feel it necessary to bring to your attention that you...."

As the words reached my ears, my heart and my mind were paralyzed with disbelief. These people with whom I shared a love/trust relationship had found it necessary to meet, clandestinely, without me. Men who had been able to bring their concerns to me privately, or openly in scheduled meetings had chosen this secretive route, but why?

Thinking back I realize I never shared with them the renewed sense of vision and direction for the church. I have regretted the fact that the church was robbed of the benefit of a progressive vision because I was blindsided and paralyzed.

Surprise Tends to Generate Confusion

The Jezebel spirit uses surprise to bring confusion into the situation or circumstance you are dealing with, and it does this through people who want to gain or maintain control. When we are relating to one another in the body of Christ, shrouded with confusion it is a perfect smoke screen for the Jezebel spirit to launch an attack.

When We Know What We Are Looking For

The modus operandi of the Jezebel spirit is identifiable. When we recognize the Jezebelic spirit's m.o. we can take the necessary steps to stop the attack.

CHAPTER FIVE

The Warning Signs of Jezebelic Activity

For you, brethren, have been called to liberty; only do not use liberty as an opportunity for the flesh, but through love serve one another. For all the law is fulfilled in one word, even in this: "You shall love your neighbor as yourself." But if you bite and devour one another, beware lest you be consumed by one another! I say then: Walk in the Spirit, and you shall not fulfill the lust of the flesh.

Galatians 5:13-16

The characteristics and nature of the Jezebel spirit's attack are warning signs. In Chapter Four we looked at the modus operandi of the Jezebel spirit. In this chapter we will be looking at the warning signs. Warning signs are very helpful, especially if you are traveling into an unknown area. I'm so appreciative of the warning signs we see on the highways here in the United States. I'm thankful that the people who are responsible for highway safety have taken their job seriously enough to place warning signs at just the right location to prevent accidents. Warning signs make the trip safe and enjoyable. They are, to some extent, responsible for the successful completion of our journey. But warning signs are only valuable if you observe them and proceed accordingly. This is true also with life in the church.

Characteristics Are the Signs

Every identifiable entity has its own characteristics. Characteristics are distinguishing attributes. As we lay the foundation for this chapter about the characteristics and nature of the Jezebel spirit, you will see that warning signs are synonymous with these characteristics.

What we will see as characteristics of the Jezebel spirit will also be characteristics of our carnal nature. The reason for this is simple. It is our carnal nature that the Jezebel spirit chooses to use as a seedbed for destruction. Consequently, when the Jezebelic activity manifests, couched in our carnal nature, it will take on the characteristics of our carnal nature.

Works of the Flesh

Chapter Three focused on the carnal nature. We identified that nature as the flesh. Since the Jezebel spirit plants the seeds of destruction in our carnal nature, it is important for us to see what the Scriptures say are works of the flesh. It is these very works that will be manifest as the Jezebel spirit launches its attack.

> For the flesh lusts against the Spirit, and the Spirit against the flesh; and these are contrary to one another, so that you do not do the things that you wish. But if you are led by the Spirit, you are not under the law. Now the works of the flesh are evident, which are: adultery, fornication,

uncleanness, lewdness, idolatry, sorcery, hatred, contentions, jealousies, outbursts of wrath, selfish ambitions, dissensions, heresies, envy, murders, drunkenness, revelries, and the like; of which I tell you beforehand, just as I also told you in time past, that those who practice such things will not inherit the kingdom of God.

Galatians 5:17-21

This scripture lists eighteen areas that are identified as works of the flesh and can be related directly to the attack of the Jezebel spirit. When you see the works of the flesh operating in the church, watch out! You are about to be "blind-sided."

This is exactly the scenario that the Jezebelic spirit is looking for. Once a person is moving in the flesh, he or she is no longer moving by the spirit. The spirit and the flesh are contrary to one another.

Don't you know that when you offer yourselves to someone to obey him as slaves, you are slaves to the one whom you obey - whether you are slaves to sin, which leads to death, or to obedience, which leads to righteousness?

Romans 6:16 NIV

For the sinful nature desires what is contrary to the Spirit, and the Spirit what is contrary to the sinful nature. They are in conflict[1] with each other, so that you do not do what you want.

Galatians 5:17 NIV

Flesh Out of Control

The Holy Spirit has specific functions that result in benefits to us as we relate to Him and He to us. He is in constant communication mode bearing witness with our spirit, teaching, leading, guiding[2]. When the soul (our heart, the center of our being, our life and mind) yields to the flesh rather than the spirit, the soul is no longer under the influence of the Holy Spirit. Our soul is being impacted and manipulated by the desires of the flesh. This is flesh out of control and available to be subject to the Jezebelic spirit.

Keep in mind this truth: If the attack of the enemy is by means other than the carnal nature of man, then it is not Jezebelic activity. However, since we understand that the carnal nature is the place where the Jezebel spirit plants seeds for destruction, to correctly identify Jezebelic activity, we must look for evidence of a carnal nature [3] out of control.

The Works of the Flesh

Sexual Immorality[4], The flesh is very weak in this area and the Jezebel spirit loves to use the seduction of harlotry, adultery, and fornication as a way to accomplish its purpose with harlotry.

Impurity[5] **and Debauchery** The Jezebel spirit is looking to use an individual who is morally unclean to try to thwart the purposes of God. Moral uncleanness can be described as licentiousness, lasciviousness, and any lust that drives the flesh.

Idolatry.[7], Our flesh is enticed to worship images and to practice idolatry by making things and individuals into idols. Our flesh can turn good things into idols, things such as ministry, education, philosophy, and heritage, or it could be a specific theology or even the next move of God.

Witchcraft.[8], Because the flesh is impatient, it is tempted to use witchcraft to accomplish its desire; in its simplest form, witchcraft is control/manipulation.

Hatred.[9], The flesh manifesting hatred can control people, situations, and events. Since we aspire to a life of peace, people allow manipulation to avoid a hostile environment. Hatred is a powerful form of manipulation.

Discord.[10], You know the ones: people who love to debate and bring strife and contentiousness into the arena, just to control the outcome.

Jealousy[11], Out of the root of jealousy the flesh sometimes wants to emulate another. At times the flesh will hold malice toward another as a result of jealousy. At other times jealous flesh expresses itself with indignation.

Fits of Rage.[12], The flesh will let itself go with fierce indignation, escalating to a fit of rage. The flesh does not mind exercising wrath when it is enraged.

Selfish Ambition.[13], The flesh will move itself to a place of establishing factions to gain support for its position. It can bring great strife and become very contentious.

Dissensions.[14], The flesh can bring about disunity through dissention, division, and strife. This becomes very useful to the Jezebelic spirit.

Factions.[15], The Jezebel spirit loves instability, and factions bring instability. Factions are created in a variety of ways, but they always begin with a lack of unity. They are sometimes accomplished through heresy and a sectarian disposition.

Envy.[16], When envy reaches maturity, it manifests itself through ill will and jealousy. It is evil to desire ill will toward another.

Drunkenness.[17], The flesh has a weakness for intoxication, the state of not seeing clearly. This word is speaking of a state of being. In other words, some intoxicant has been used to bring about intoxication or drunkenness. We would make a mistake to limit intoxicants to alcohol. An individual can become intoxicated with power, money, vanity, self-worth, and the list goes on. The Jezebel spirit works best to move its agenda when the flesh is intoxicated.

Orgies.[18], The flesh is prone to being out of control, and this word indicates the flesh being completely out of control, even to the point of reveling and rioting.

The Effect of Works of the Flesh

People who manifest the works of the flesh are dangerous and need to be confronted. The Bible speaks of their activity and its effect in the book of 2 Peter:

> But these, like natural brute beasts made to be caught and destroyed, speak evil of the things they do not understand, and will utterly perish in their own corruption, and will receive the wages of unrighteousness, as those who count it pleasure to carouse in the daytime. They are spots and blemishes, carousing in their own deceptions while they feast with you, having eyes full of adultery and that cannot cease from sin, **enticing unstable souls**. They have a heart trained in covetous practices, and are accursed children. They have forsaken the right way and gone

astray, following the way of Balaam the son of
Beor, who loved the wages of unrighteousness.

2 Peter 2:12-15

Their own corruption will bring them to a fatal end.
Their end is predictable, but notice the ones who are being
affected, those unstable souls. It is imperative that we exercise wisdom and actively pursue identifying and dealing
with Jezebelic activity in the church.

What to Look For

In order for us to exercise caution and move with
wisdom, it is necessary to know what to look for. While
moving in the flesh, people manifest certain characteristics
that are identifiable and deserve our attention. We should
use caution when relating to people who are known by these
characteristics:

- Refuses to admit guilt or wrong
- Uses people to accomplish their agenda
- Withholds information
- Speaks in confusion
- Volunteers for anything
- Lies
- Ignores people
- Never gives credit or shows gratitude
- Criticizes everyone
- One-upmanship
- Sequesters information
- Uses information
- Talks incessantly
- Spiritualizes everything
- Is insubordinate
- Is pushy and dominating
- Is clairvoyant

- Uses the element of surprise for their own benefit
- Sows seeds of discord
- Commands attention
- Attempts to make you look like a Jezebel
- Insinuates disapproval
- Is a know-it-all
- Is ambitious
- Extraordinary gift giving
- Is extremely independent
- Is religious
- Hides

This is not an exhaustive list; you may be able to add others and you should.

When I go through this list while teaching in a seminar setting on overcoming the Jezebel spirit, attendees begin to see these things both in themselves and others. You might be going through the same process now. May I encourage you that it is not the time to indict yourself or others. There is still another important part of the process that will allow you to know the difference between simply moving in the flesh and inciting Jezebelic activity. While we recognize that both issues need to be addressed, it is necessary to discern the difference. (See Chapter Fifteen, "Confronting the Jezebel spirit.")

Becoming Part of the Solution

My hope, as you read this chapter, is that you become aware of actions that are rooted in our flesh (carnal nature). When we see the evidence of these things in our own actions, it is time to repent, returning to the safety of allowing the Holy Spirit to lead our spirit.

There is therefore now no condemnation to those who are in Christ Jesus, who do not walk according to the flesh, but according to the Spirit.

Romans 8:1

If we are not willing to repent, we must question if our actions may be robbing the church of the opportunity to fulfill the purposes of God. **We just might be the problem, an instrument of the Jezebel spirit.**

Dedication to Pastors

From this point forward this book is dedicated to pastors and church leaders who have suffered through the attack of the Jezebel spirit. The road called Church History is littered with many who have fallen under this devastating attack of Satan that seeks to destroy the purpose of God. Ministering to pastors and church leaders has allowed me to see the hurt, pain, discouragement, and depression that come as a result of the attack. The effect of the attack is so devastating that it becomes impossible for its victims to see clearly the vision that is desperately needed for ministry and to continue in what God has called them to. That is exactly what happened to Elijah.

Broom Tree Pastors

Now Ahab told Jezebel everything Elijah had done and how he had killed all the prophets with the sword. So Jezebel sent a messenger to Elijah to say, "May the gods deal with me, be it ever so severely, if by this time tomorrow I do not make your life like that of one of them." Elijah was afraid and ran for his life. When he came to Beersheba in Judah, he left his servant there, while he himself went a day's journey into the desert. He came to a broom tree, sat down under it and prayed that he might die. "I have had enough, LORD," he said. "Take my life; I am no better than my ancestors."

1 Kings 19:1-4 NIV

Something in these few words from Jezebel caused Elijah to run into the wilderness. It is obvious that there was more involved than mere words. These words had such a devastating effect that the same man who had stood on Mount Carmel is now under a broom tree. I have met many pastors over the years who are trying to pastor their church from under a broom tree, being held hostage by depression and despair, no longer able to function, and just like Elijah, desiring only to be released from their plight.

This Book on Overcoming the Attack

Out of these experiences I have come to see God's wisdom in the design of His church, not only to stand against the attack but also to be positioned in such a way that it never has a foothold. His design is for us to be overcomers, standing victoriously at the end of the battle. I don't pretend to have the last word on this topic; however, I am convinced that God has shown me true principles that need to be embraced by the church. I remember having a conversation with Bernard Evans, President of Elim Fellowship, a man whom I highly esteem as an elder in my life. We were talking about church constitutions when he made a very profound statement. "Church constitutions are written in times of peace for times of war." He was explaining the necessity of writing a church constitution from that perspective in order that it would stand the test of a local church going through difficult times. Another principle I want to point out is the necessity to prepare ahead of time for what is inevitable in every church — that is, Satan's attack against the purpose of God.

Caution and Precaution

Caution is a word that applies when you are about to venture into an area that holds an element of danger or harm in some way. It means to take warning. When you are on a highway going 65 miles per hour and you approach a sharp curve, you often see a sign cautioning you to slow down. *Precaution* is an extremely important word that is directly related to caution. Precaution is what you did at the brake shop before you left on your trip. Without the benefit of precaution it is impossible to heed the sign cautioning you to slow down.

It is necessary to embrace the wisdom of precaution when it comes to the inevitable attack of the Jezebel spirit. Taking precaution is having in place a God-ordained plan to deal with the inevitable attack; precaution involves preparing beforehand to stand against what will surely be our experience. Knowing this truth, it is foolish not to take the necessary steps to embrace God's design for the church to be victorious. His design is clearly seen in the Scriptures.

Vision and Structure

God has given the church two basic foundational elements in His design: Vision and Structure. Both are necessary if we are going to deal with and ward off the attack of the Jezebel spirit.

In the remaining chapters we will look at specific church ministries with the intention of bringing insight to the attack of the Jezebel spirit, and how to deal with it from a pastor's perspective. You will discover that, in each case, the foundation for development and success of the ministry is **vision and structure.**

The Hinge

The word hinge is defined as anything on which matters turn or depend; a hinge is the cardinal point or principal. In the case of **vision and structure** the hinge is "dying to self." Let's consider again this key Scripture.

> If you have any encouragement from being united with Christ, if any comfort from his love, if any fellowship with the Spirit, if any tenderness and compassion, then make my joy complete by being like-minded, having the same love, being one in spirit and purpose. Do nothing out of selfish ambition or vain conceit, but in humility consider others better than yourselves. Each of you should look not only to your own interests, but also to the interests of others. Your attitude should be the same as that of Christ Jesus: Who, being in very nature God, did not consider equality with God something to be grasped, but made himself nothing, taking the very nature of a servant, being made in human likeness. And being found in appearance as a man, he humbled himself and became obedient to death - even death on a cross!
>
> Philippians 2:1-8 NIV

In this text Paul speaks of the necessity to die to one's self. His admonishment to us is that we should do nothing out of selfish ambition or vain conceit, but in humility consider others better than ourselves. As we embrace and develop **vision and structure** for the local church, every individual will be challenged and required to die to self.

My Prayer

My prayer for you, Pastor, is that you succeed in dealing with the attack of the Jezebel spirit in the church as you serve God's purpose. I pray that God will grant you wisdom and knowledge as you stand in the place of being His under-shepherd to lead His people. I pray also for His healing touch in the recovery process for you and your congregation as you experience deliverance from Jezebelic activity.

I trust you will benefit from this book as you face the challenge that is certain.

In His Love,
Don Richter

For the rest of you who read this dedication to pastors, please join me in this prayer. As you read this book, you will also discover vital truths that can help you understand the nature of the Jezebelic attack, so that you can partner with your pastor and fellow Christians to achieve total victory in this area of spiritual warfare.

When I was being trained for a managerial position, I was taught this principle: "Individuals are either a part of the problem or a part of the solution." At first, I did not understand the fullness of this truth. However, when I was overseeing the work of three hundred employees, this truth became very evident. My desire is that each of us will become a part of the solution and not be identified as part of the problem.

CHAPTER SIX

God's Design for Success

Unless the LORD builds the house, they labor
in vain who build it; unless the LORD guards
the city, the watchman stays awake in vain.

Psalms 127:1

If the church is going to overcome the attack of the
Jezebel spirit, it must be able to stop the attack. We can
never prevent the attack, which is initiated as a part of
Satan's ongoing strategy to cause the church to be dysfunctional. However, we can stop it. There are two elements in
God's design for the church that must be in place to stop the
attack of the Jezebel spirit: **vision and structure**. A church
lacking these elements will be in continual turmoil, missing
the purposes of God as a local congregation.

Vision and Structure

In the following chapters we will focus on these two
crucial areas: "vision" (Chapter Seven), and "structure"

(Chapter Eight). I will discuss these areas in the context of recognizing the need to present and embrace a **clear vision** and a **viable structure** in the local church.

If these areas are undefined or not clearly defined, the church will live in a vulnerable and insecure environment and have difficulty connecting to the whole body of Christ. There is no way for the people of God to move forward victoriously if they are not aware of or do not embrace the vision and structure of the church they attend.

It is God's design to accomplish His purposes in and through the church. A developing new church or an older established church has a common need, which is to be vision-driven with a viable structure.

The Foundation for Dealing With Issues

Every church has issues. Often these issues exist because people choose to walk in the flesh. Issues are a part of church life. It may not be as obvious to the people in the church as it is to the leadership of the church, and especially to the pastor. Please do not misunderstand my statement. I realize that the people in your church do not walk in the flesh all the time. However, I also realize that all the people, in every church, walk in the flesh part of the time. The result is the constant possibility of the Jezebel spirit gaining a foothold in the local church.

The **vision** and **structure** of the church form the foundation on which all the issues concerning purpose and discipline are settled. This foundation is essential when it comes to dealing with Jezebelic activity.

A New Church Adventure

As I slid into the pew, my heart was racing; I had arrived early, thank God. What a blessing it had been to have our Realtor, Joe, meet the moving van yesterday to help us unload.

I'd had such apprehension about moving all the way across the country. Somehow, I just knew Joe was a Christian when he took me to see the house. There was not anything I could see or hear, but I just knew it in my spirit, somehow.

Can you believe it? I've been here less than 24 hours and I'm sitting in New Covenant Church, thanks to Joe's invitation and directions.

I knew when I left Norwich, Connecticut and Grace Community it would be an adventure to find a new church home. Halleluiah it has already begun! I'm so excited; I can't wait to see what God has for me. He knows the desires of my heart, just to serve Him and see the lost saved.

Leaving Grace Community was so hard, but I know that God has the perfect place for me. "God help me see what this church is all about. God, I wonder if this is the place where you intend for me to put my hand to the plow and continue to labor in your vineyard."

Embracing and Connecting

Many begin church life much like Joe's new friend, finding themselves displaced for one reason or another, looking for a church home that will be God's choice, a place to connect and serve as they grow spiritually.

However, there are others, those who have come to know Jesus as Lord through the ministry of your church, and I hope your church has a significant number of them.

These two groups of people have something in common. They both need to embrace and connect with the **vision and structure** of the church they attend. Without that connection they will be living in an increasing state of randomness. The result will be utter and total collapse of their potential to become a viable part of the body of Christ.

Not an Option; It Is Mandatory

We are all challenged with the responsibility of embracing the **vision** and **structure** of the church. It is not an option; it is mandatory if we are going to be the people God has called us to be.

In some cases people don't attend church, or they attend many churches, because of their inability to embrace a local church's vision and structure. This is not God's design or intention. If we choose to disconnect from the church for whatever reason, we are also disconnecting from the very thing that God has set in place for our growth and maturity.

It is in being a part of the fabric of the local church that we find the gifts God gave to the church, for the maturing of the saints, that they may be equipped for the work of the ministry.

> And He Himself gave some to be apostles, some prophets, some evangelists, and some pastors and teachers, for the equipping of the saints for the work of ministry, for the edifying of the body of Christ, till we all come to the unity of the faith and the knowledge of the Son of God, to a perfect man, to the measure of the stature of the fullness of Christ; that we should no longer be children, **tossed to and fro and carried about with every wind of doctrine, by the trickery of men, in the cunning craftiness of deceitful plotting,** but, speaking the truth in love, may grow up in all things into Him who is the head - Christ - from whom the whole body, joined and knit together by what every joint supplies, according to the effective working by which every part does its share, causes growth of the body for the edifying of itself in love.
>
> Ephesians 4:11-16

Pay special attention to verse fourteen as it relates to Jezebelic activity in the church. The Jezebel spirit loves to cause spiritually immature people to be tossed to and fro, subject to the trickery of men.

The resources for spiritual development are found within the church; these are the ministry gifts given by God to facilitate growth, maturity, and stability. The inability to embrace the **vision** and **structure** of the church will leave you ill equipped to be able to stand against the enemy, particularly Jezebelic activity in the church.

Do Not Be Drawn In

My heart goes out to those reading this book who have been wounded by Jezebelic activity. Perhaps you have chosen to escape the hurt and discouragement you experienced in a local church by leaving. Maybe you have decided, "The best thing for me is to get away from the source of the hurt." Still others of you have become disillusioned and have made the tragic choice of not becoming a part of a local church again. I urge you to reconsider your decision. You may have walked right into the ploy of the Jezebel spirit, and so now you are dysfunctional in relation to the purposes of God in your life. Don't let yourself be drawn into this place of being disconnected with God's design and purpose for the church and for you.

CHAPTER SEVEN

God's Vision and the Local Church

Where there is no revelation, the people cast off restraint.

Proverbs 29:18

Where there is no vision, the people perish.

Proverbs 29:18 KJV

And He spoke a parable to them: "Can the blind lead the blind? Will they not both fall into the ditch?"

Luke 6:39

God's will holds within it a vision to accomplish His purposes. God does not lead His church blindly nor does He lead indiscriminately. It is this very fact that enables a sense of security and destiny to grow within the church.

Discovering the Vision

If you are a pastor, have you discovered the vision that God has for the church you are leading? **Discovering the vision** is a profound truth regarding the vision of the local church. Too many times church leaders do not understand that God does not mean for us to **develop a vision** for the local church. His desire is for us to **discover the vision**. This is such an important difference.

Exploring the Past

Lois and I scrambled up the ladder leading to what should have been the hayloft in an old barn; our hearts were pounding with excitement. The barn was on the Lattimer property. The farm had a rich history, having been part of the Underground Railroad that was the way to freedom for countless numbers of slaves as they passed through New York on their way to Canada. We were breathless and speechless when we lifted the trap door to the loft. Not from the climb, but from what our eyes beheld!

We were exploring property that we were planning to purchase. We were not able to buy the whole farm, but we did acquire a large portion of the land. We were certain that God gave us the opportunity and provision to purchase the property. One of the deciding factors was what we discovered while exploring this old barn. On the side of the barn was written "I Am" in thirty-six-inch letters. The paint was very faded, but we could easily make out the words that pointed our hearts toward God.

The property was a part of the estate of Mr. Lattimer, who left among his belongings a letter he had written to God shortly before he died. In this letter he thanked God for the good life He had given him and his wife. He also thanked God for his brothers and sisters. Mr. Lattimer was an orphan; the brothers and sisters he was thankful for were the fellow Christians he knew as a result of knowing his heavenly

Father. His letter also expressed his joy and delight in dedicating this property to God. His prayer was that whoever owned the property after him would be as blessed as he was and that they would use the property to glorify Him.

We purchased the land, unaware that within ten years we would be in fulltime ministry, building a church on nine acres of the property. Many times, as we saw the church grow and become fruitful over the years, my mind went back to that day of discovery. Let me continue my story of what we found in the hayloft.

We were amazed to discover the loft had been used as a church decades earlier! It might have been part of the Underground Railroad. It was still set up as a meeting room, and we could see where the preacher stood to deliver the Word of God. The area was large enough to hold fifty to sixty people. The loft area was filled with a quiet reverence. As the sunlight streamed through the spaces between the vertical barn siding, it caused the mist in the air to glow softly. We could sense the presence of God. Lois and I found ourselves speaking to one another in a whisper so as not to interfere with the sanctity of this place. In my spirit I could hear the "amens" to sermons gone by and wondered what happened in the lives of the people who had gathered here.

Years later I realized that as we embraced an unfolding vision for the church that we saw founded and built on that land, we were not **developing** the vision; we were **discovering** the vision. That day when we climbed the ladder, we discovered not only a meeting area where a church had gathered in decades gone by, but we also discovered the first part of an unfolding vision of God for a church to flourish on that land. What a joy it was to participate in this!

We concluded we had come to join God's vision for this land and this community. We didn't come with our own agenda; we came looking for His agenda.

I have learned that the initial step in having a local church vision is discovery. **The vision is not developed—it is discovered.**

In reality, we as leaders are in error if we are not committed to discovering God's vision rather than trying to develop one of our own. When we are the initiator of a vision, the vision lacks integrity.

Waiting to Be Discovered

Many pastors approach the matter of local church vision from the wrong perspective and in some cases with wrong motive. Local church vision is waiting to be discovered. Too often we fail to see that God has a vision for the local church, and we need to discover it.

If we were to answer the call to pastor in a community and approach this call as though God never had a thought or plan before we arrived on the scene, we would be guilty of arrogance and shortsightedness. To think we bring a local-church vision to a community, as opposed to seeking God for the vision He has already determined for that community, is a wrong perspective.

This is a challenge; it is easier to function in what we know than to wait on God for what He desires. Sometimes we are guilty of doing something just to make an impression. Being a people-pleaser keeps our critics quiet; however, we are not pastoring to keep critics quiet. We are pastoring the church to see the purposes of God fulfilled in the lives of the believers and the communities where they live. We can do that only when we have discovered His vision for the church we pastor.

Wrong Motive

This little church had been through enough. It had taken many years getting to this stage of development and growth. The departure of the founding pastor was a shock.

However, he left them with **vision** and **structure** for reaching their community.

We received a call from Fred; he heard there was an opportunity here for someone who is called to pastor. As we talked, Fred shared that he has a vision for a cutting-edge, praying church. His ministry, as he sees it, is to develop a prayer network, traveling and speaking. He expressed the need for a place to develop a unique prayer model that he could duplicate in other places.

Too often leaders have a personal vision with their own agenda for accomplishing that vision. They will choose to pastor a church to facilitate their agenda without regard to the vision God has for that church and community. Clearly this is wrong motivation and does not encompass seeking with integrity, a local church vision.

Viable Church Vision

The Faith Gap

It was years ago that the "faith-gap" principle first challenged me. We were having a series of meetings with Dr. Phil Derstine of Bradenton Christian Retreat as our speaker. He introduced us to this principle that I have come to embrace in all areas of ministry. Phil showed us a line graph with two lines representing our resources and our vision. He began the graph with the line representing our vision being higher than the line representing our resources. The difference between these two lines represents our faith gap. The faith gap is the evidence that we are placing our trust in God for His provision for the vision He has given to us. He continued to chart the graph to a point where our resources line gradually increased, crossing and then spiking higher than the vision line. He said that at the point where our resources are greater than our vision, we will have become an institution, no longer experiencing a faith gap, or a dependence on God for His provision.

If the vision of the local church does not demand a faith gap, I question if we have discovered God's vision for that local church. Some think we should not embrace a vision that we are not sure we can afford. This philosophy excludes the need to depend on God for His provision.

What a Tragedy

Those who are governed only by what is in their hand will never see the potential they have in His hand. What keeps them in this place of limited potential is the sense of security that comes from not dealing with the unknown—in other words, not having to exercise faith for the vision they carry. What a tragedy!

> But without faith it is impossible to please Him, for he who comes to God must believe that He is, and that He is a rewarder of those who diligently seek Him.
>
> Hebrews 11:6

Weak or Non-Existent Vision

Often the local church is subject to a weak or non-existent vision. If the vision is to be viable, it is necessary that the vision be set in place with clarity and definition. Another term that expresses this process well is **casting the vision**. A local church vision has no opportunity to be realized if it is poorly presented and established. Ambiguous, undefined details of a vision will only lead to confusion. Confusion is like fuel when the church is under the Jezebelic attack.

Pastors must accept the responsibility of discovering, processing, and **casting the vision** for the local church. The local church must accept the responsibility of embracing the vision that has been processed and set in place with integrity. Our desire should be to marry the vision of the local church and become a viable part of seeing its fullest potential reached. If we will do that, then we will see and know the Lord's blessing in our lives and in the community where we live.

If the vision is to accomplish all that God intends, it must bear all the attributes of a healthy local church vision. In order for leaders to **cast the vision** with confidence, it is necessary to embrace the characteristics and dynamics inherent in a viable local church vision.

Vision With the Wrong Focus

Institutionalized by Historical Identification

I think of the Israelites leaving Egypt and the necessity for them to follow God each step of the way. God gave Moses the vision, the purpose, and the objective: "the promised land." God established this vision based on the past, the present, and the future of His people.

Moses could have cast the vision for the Israelites embracing only their history. The vision would have been "we are the people of the God of our fathers, Abraham, Isaac, and Jacob," with no further understanding of their destiny and purpose. Their hope for fulfilling God's purpose would have been lost in a vision that has reached its end. Some churches are like that; their identity is based solely on their history, having a sense of "we have arrived and there is nothing more we need " rather than, "we are on our way to God's intended objective and purpose."

Pastors will sometimes seek identity in their history, not embracing their future. In so doing they miss what God has intended for the local church. In order for the Israelites to reach that intended objective and realize their purpose, it was necessary for them to take one step at a time, with each step being revealed at the necessary time to move them toward the predetermined objective couched in the vision God gave Moses. It was up to Moses to discover, impart, and implement the vision each step of the way.

Vision Focused on the Next Best Thing

Moses could have cast a vision based only on their current circumstances and experiences, i.e., we are "the wandering people," practicing the presence of God in the wilderness. Having no sense of their history or their intended future would hinder them in fulfilling God's intent and purpose. We see churches whose vision only places value on the contemporary, lacking the benefit of a vision that is shaped over time, rooted in the history of a faithful God blended with His promised destiny and a clear and present leading.

I see such a church as one that is going in circles. It has nothing to move it out of the state of inertia. A church with this perspective is impeded in its progress because the people are held hostage by what they perceive as the "next best thing." Many times they will embrace a movement with an intensity and passion to the point of losing their identity. A vision that is rooted in history, with a motivation toward destiny, will actively pursue the next step that takes them from a cyclical pattern to a linear direction.

Tunnel Vision

I remember a teacher in school who wanted us to experience what people with tunnel vision experience. He instructed us to take a piece of paper and roll it into a cylindrical shape and then bring it to one eye and look through while the other eye was closed. The result was that we could see the object of our focus but could not see anything that was going on around us. His experiment caused us to know the handicap of tunnel vision. The reality of tunnel vision exists in the spiritual realm as well as the natural.

Moses could have cast a vision looking only to the future. This would have been "spiritual tunnel vision." "We are the people of the Promised Land." A vision that is based only on that which is to come misses the fruit of the process. The Israelites learned to trust God day by day in the current circumstances of their life, preparing them for the future promise of God, their destiny.

Some leaders **cast a vision** that has been discovered through spiritual tunnel vision. A church whose vision is focused only on the future will miss the next step in the process of preparation. A viable vision that embraces the future does not divorce itself from the foundation of its historical roots or the current maturing process connected to the present leading of God in this day.

Attributes of a Viable Church Vision

Local Church Vision Is Progressive
The vision of God is progressive and needs to be received and imparted as such. This means that what is initially seen and understood is the beginning, not the end.

Sometimes we see and have knowledge of an overall direction and objective. However, that objective will not be realized unless we continue to receive daily revelation. Moses knew the final destiny, not the details; they were given along the way. Leaders need to be seeking God for the necessary adjustments to stay on course.

Embracing the Progressive Vision
Over the last ten years I have watched Elim Bible Institute go through an amazing transformation. Paul Johansson, President of EBI, is a visionary. God puts people like him in places where strong visionary leadership is needed. No one, including Paul, knew all the details of this transformation. As I observed the ongoing changes, I was so

impressed by Paul's tenacity and confidence as he walked out the vision for the school. One of the key characteristics of the vision was its progressive nature. The success of the vision unfolding was due to Paul's commitment to embrace that nature, trusting God.

The receiving and imparting of a progressive vision is evidence of a healthy local church living to please God. A church that is willing to receive adjustments along the way demonstrates a walk of faith. The Bible is clear about people who walk in faith.

> But without faith it is impossible to please Him, for he who comes to God must believe that He is, and that He is a rewarder of those who diligently seek Him.
>
> Hebrews 11:6

If it is impossible to please Him without faith, then it is possible to please Him with faith.

Constant Change Brings Critics

The local church vision is constantly in a state of change, because the vision is not revealed all at one time. Since this is a reality, the pressure from the people in the church comes in two ways. One way is, "Pastor, there is something wrong with what we are doing. Every program we start has not continued. We have been so blessed but nothing seems to last." The other pressure is, "Pastor, do we need to change this? If it is not broken, why fix it, why not leave it as it is? You're making changes means more work for us." Both of these things are true; nothing continues as it was and changes mean work.

Do Not Be Caught Stranded

Every time the presence of God moved, the people of Israel needed to move. I can imagine there were some who complained that they never stayed put. Yet another group probably complained that every time they moved, it meant work to pack up not only their personal belongings, but their assigned portion of the tabernacle.

Once the vision was imparted and instructions given concerning how to embrace the vision, the responsibility to do so remained with each individual. In the wilderness, the pillar of fire and pillar of cloud (the Presence of God) moved.[1]. Those who would remain in God's will needed to move with Him. I am sure, as I consider the nature of people, there were those who complained and rebelled against what was imparted as the vision of God for them. Regardless of how clearly the vision was imparted and implemented, I believe there were those who just didn't get it.

Pastors Need to Be Relentless

Pastor, there are times that we do all we can possibly do to make the vision clear and viable, and still there are those who just don't get it. I want to encourage you not to let them remain unattached to the vision. If they do they will become a potential stronghold for the enemy to launch a Jezebelic attack in the church. Be relentless in **casting the vision**. Write it down so those who read it may run with it.

> Then the LORD answered me and said: "Write the vision and make it plain on tablets, that he may run who reads it. For the vision is yet for an appointed time; but at the end it will speak, and it will not lie. Though it tarries, wait for it; because it will surely come, it will not tarry."
>
> Habakkuk 2:2-3

Pastor, I encourage you not to grow weary of seeking God for the necessary changes and adjustments as you live out what He has for the church each day. We must not become lazy in our pursuit of God's vision with its ever-changing revelation for the local church. A church that does not experience continual development is in a quagmire, living in its yesterdays, not looking for the adjustments that will bring it to God's intended purpose and objective.

Local Church Vision Is Universally Related

It sounds like a dichotomy: that the local church vision must be universally related to God's vision for the universal church. It is not really a dichotomy; God has established His church with clear purpose and commission.

Too many times local churches become so ingrown in vision that they miss the global aspect of what God is doing. This is when we begin to hear statements that are not supportive of embracing God's objective and purpose for the church globally, i.e., "we are a family church, not a missions church," or, "we are a discipling church, not soul winners."

Church Vision Must Embrace God's Objectives and Purposes

God's objectives and purposes are seen clearly in His great commission.

> "Go therefore and make disciples of all the nations, baptizing them in the name of the Father and of the Son and of the Holy Spirit, "teaching them to observe all things that I have commanded you; and lo, I am with you always, even to the end of the age." Amen.
>
> Matthew 28:19-20

"But you shall receive power when the Holy
Spirit has come upon you; and you shall be
witnesses to Me in Jerusalem, and in all Judea
and Samaria, and to the end of the earth."

Acts 1:8

If the vision we are embracing does not relate universally to God's intent and purpose for the church, then we
have missed His best for us.

One of the identifying characteristics of our relationship
with God is that we are being sent.

As You sent Me into the world, I also have sent
them into the world.

John 17:18

Jesus references our being sent to the way He was sent.
The question is, how was He sent? He was sent in love and
in power with purpose and intent.

For God so loved the world that He gave His
only begotten Son, that whoever believes in
Him should not perish but have everlasting life.

John 3:16

There is no doubt that He was sent in love and with
intent and purpose:

Behold, I give you the authority to trample on
serpents and scorpions, and over all the power
of the enemy, and nothing shall by any means
hurt you.

Luke 10:19

He was sent with power, and He is sending us with power as well. He is sending the church with love and power, with specific intent and purpose.

A healthy local church vision is universally, directly, related to His sending us to the nations with intent and purpose. His design and desire is for the local church to have a Kingdom effect in its community, region, and the world as the people of God, the fullness[2] of Him in the face of the earth.

Vision Establishes Direction and Position

Vision very clearly establishes direction. The first thing people want to know concerning the local church is, "what is this church all about and where are we going?" These are the right questions for people who are looking to connect with the vision and structure of the church. Leaders are generally threatened by these questions if they don't have a clear vision and structure set in place.

There is an inherent perspective in the kingdom of God, one of "we have not arrived yet." This perspective is a reality whether we recognize it or not. The vision of the local church should be clear in its direction as it pursues the destination that God has ordained.

Most times we think of the physical destination. However, we learn from the Exodus that God had in mind, in addition to a physical destination, a spiritual positioning as well for His people, in order that His desires should come to pass.

For Moses, the destination in the physical was the Promised Land. However, the vision of God that Moses imparted addressed the spiritual aspect of their relationship with God as well; a spiritual positioning, if you will, so that they could be successful in the mission for which they had been sent.

The vision for the local church must be as comprehensive as the vision Moses carried for God's people. It must establish the direction of the local church in the physical as well as establishing spiritual positioning.

There are many reasons that pastors cast a vision not including both of these aspects. However, all of those reasons are rooted in the perspective the pastor has for the church. It could be that the pastor is more concerned about the physical aspect, so he prays continually for the next step in the building project, or the property to be purchased, or the number of people in the local church.

I once heard the testimony of a prominent pastor as he shared his shortcomings so that we might learn and grow from them. He shared how he came up with a program that would grow the numbers in the church. He began to give away table settings of dishes and flatware every time someone brought a new person to the church. He said the church began to grow very rapidly. One day as he was thanking God for the uncommon growth, God spoke to him and said, "If you use fleshly means to grow a church of 6,000, then you will have a church of 6,000 fleshly people. Is that what you want?"

Leaders must pursue a comprehensive vision for the church that embraces both the physical and the spiritual dimensions.

Vision Determines Discipline

The vision of the local church not only establishes direction and position, but it also dictates the activity. This activity can be described as the discipline of the local church. People who become part of the local church desire to become part of the activity of the church. If the vision is not clear, then the activity is not focused. Perhaps a more descriptive word would be confusion. So, what generally happens is, "it's every man for himself," and the activity in the church becomes non-productive regarding the purpose God has for that local congregation.

People who embrace the vision of the local church will be found sacrificially pouring themselves into the work of the ministry. There will be an abundance of faithful servants to carry out each area of responsibility. Leaders who complain that there is never enough help should examine, once again, their success of imparting a viable vision for the church. There are plenty of workers if we present a clear vision for them to embrace.

This is clearly seen in the day-to-day operation of the Exodus of the people of Israel. Faithful people served the vision as they fulfilled their commitment to move every aspect of the tabernacle when God said, "Let us move."

This is what leaders are looking for: faithful people who have embraced the vision so that when God says, "Let us move," each area of responsibility will be covered.

Local Church Vision Establishes Purpose

The vision not only establishes direction and activity, but it also establishes purpose. Every human being has the basic fundamental need of realizing purpose in his or her life. The lack of realized purpose is the root problem of many who seek counseling for their dysfunctional personal lives. Without purpose they lack confidence and stability.

The same dynamic applies to a local church congregation. If there is no identifiable purpose, people become dysfunctional. The ministry of that church will lack confidence and stability. We cannot serve effectively if we don't have the acceptance of the community where we live and serve. That acceptance is dependant on the community recognizing within the church a people of purpose, serving confidently, and demonstrating stability as we represent the fullness of Him in the face of the earth.

When a congregation understands its purpose, there will be a new level of commitment and participation in the local church vision.

Processing Local Church Vision

It is a major challenge to process the vision to a final conclusion so that it can be imparted with confidence. The vision the pastor imparts is to be without repentance or regret.

> Then Moses said, "I will now turn aside and see this great sight, why the bush does not burn." So when the LORD saw that he turned aside to look, God called to him from the midst of the bush and said, "Moses, Moses!" And he said, "Here I am." Then He said, "Do not draw near this place. Take your sandals off your feet, for the place where you stand is holy ground."
>
> Exodus 3:3-5

God has the vision before He calls a man. When Moses was attracted to the burning bush, God revealed His vision for the deliverance of His people out of Egypt. The vision was in place before Moses approached the bush. It was necessary for Moses to process the vision.

In brief God told him the objective and purpose for the release of His people. He did not give him the details. Moses embraced God's vision without knowing the details. The need to know the details of God's vision for a local church is essential for the fulfillment of the vision, *not for the embracing of it*. The details became known to Moses after his commitment to become one with the vision God was imparting.

The First Step for Processing the Vision Is to "Turn Aside"

"The Lord saw that he turned aside to look." God's vision for us always asks us to turn aside, in other words, to change directions or refocus our attention. If you are not willing to arrest your personal vision and understanding for the sake of the continual unfolding of what God is communicating, you will miss the fullness of what God has envisioned.

The flow of God's vision to Moses was dependent on Moses turning aside. It was when God saw that Moses turned aside to look that God called him. It is necessary for us to not only turn aside, but also to look or be attentive. It was at that time that God spoke to Moses. Getting your attention and having your attention are two different things. One is simply being attracted; the other is being totally captivated by what has gotten your attention. All too often we are not totally captivated by what God is showing as the vision that will accomplish His objectives. We allow distractions that weaken our position of being the people of God having purpose and destiny.

God Tests the Relationship

It is interesting to note that His initial words to Moses had nothing to do with the deliverance of the people out of Egypt. They were words that would test Moses' relationship with God.

He said, "Moses take off your sandals, for you are standing on holy ground." This was the test. The word in the Hebrew that is translated sandal is na`al,[3] and one of its primary meanings has to do with marriage. What God was saying is, "Will you marry me, Moses?" "Will you marry my Vision?"

Instant Revelation Becomes a Lifetime of Walking Out

God cannot trust His vision with someone who is not willing to marry the vision He gives. We cannot see clearly what Moses' response was, but his walking out the deliverance of God's people gives us some insight. Moses did marry the vision God had for the deliverance of His people. If we are going to accomplish all that God has for us, we must marry His vision in order to fulfill His purposes in our life and ministry.

What was expressed in a few words to Moses took forty years of processing before they entered the Promised Land. What is needed for a lifetime of walking out a vision? We must be committed to the vision that God has given in such a way that it becomes our identity. How does the vision give us identity? When we become one with something it becomes our identity.

Lois and I are married; we have become one. Our identity is as one, having been married more than forty-eight years. That is our identity; everyone who knows us sees us that way. Those who have come to know us closely know that we are totally committed to our relationship. There is not a chance that we are going to be drawn off track. Because of that commitment we are secure in our identity as one.

When we become committed to the vision that God has for us, and our identity is formed as a result of that commitment, then we become secure in what God has called us to. It is a lifetime commitment. Moses could have made other choices, but he did not. Instead, he embraced the vision and spent the remainder of his life living out the vision, becoming one of the most significant leaders in the history of God's people.

Who Am I

Many times our focus is on us who are called, rather than the One who called us.

> But Moses said to God, "Who am I that I should go to Pharaoh and bring the Israelites out of Egypt?"
>
> Exodus 3:11 NIV

When Moses questioned Him, looking at himself relative to the vision, there was doubt as to the possibility of success. Moses knew the power and authority of Pharaoh. He also knew he did not possess what was needed to persuade and influence Pharaoh to let the people go.

> And God said, "I will be with you. And this will be the sign to you that it is I who have sent you: When you have brought the people out of Egypt, you will worship God on this mountain."
> Exodus 3:12 NIV

God shifted Moses' focus to Himself as a guarantee of success. It is necessary to look to the One who not only gives the vision but also guarantees its success by His walking it out with us.

Casting the Vision

Clear Vision, Not Confusion

Local church leadership needs to cast vision with clarity and confidence. The one to do this is the pastor. He is the under-shepherd, the one who is leading the flock of God. I know that God blesses a plurality of leaders in the local church; however, from among them there will be one who walks by grace in the responsibility of an under-shepherd, the pastor. Part of his responsibility is to cast the vision for the church. He is the one who moves the flock in the direction that God has revealed.

How he determines the aspects of the vision may vary. God will use circumstances, situations, and others' input. However, the final determination is made when God confirms in the pastor's spirit the details of the vision.

When someone other than the pastor is casting the vision, confusion sets in.

I have known churches that have felt it was spiritually mature for more than just the pastor to cast the vision, thinking that many voices of leadership will bring a level of confidence in the congregation. This is a mistake; they need to hear one voice — that of their pastor — with a clear demonstration on the part of their leadership that this is the vision God has for the church.

This will establish confidence and security in the congregation. They will embrace the vision with a single-mindedness that will keep them from the destruction of the Jezebelic attack.

Birthing the Vision

Successful pastors give birth to the vision of the local church. Vision should not be imposed on a congregation. The congregation should be given the opportunity to give birth to the vision. We are the body of Christ, a living entity that has the capacity of giving birth. Local church vision is a living thing that needs to be birthed.

It is necessary to have conception in order to have a birth. Conception takes place in an intimate relationship. When someone is thinking about conceiving a baby, they don't approach a perfect stranger and propose the idea of conception. They approach the one who is closest to them, their spouse. The pastor, if married, needs to discuss the vision with his or her spouse, who is also their partner in the ministry.

I know that some who are reading this book may not be able to relate to this statement because they view themselves only as being called to ministry, but not their spouse. If you're married, you are both called. God does not call half of the relationship into ministry; He calls you both as one. Your functions in the church may vary but because you are one, the call includes you both. Therefore, whatever you are about to decide regarding the vision is going to require sacrifice and commitment. The one you are married to will be involved in that sacrifice and commitment. Allow for the opportunity for conception.

Vision and the Elders

The next level of relationships to know about the conception is family. That circle in a local church would be the elders, those who are closest to you as the pastor. When a couple conceives a child, the first ones they announce the good news to are usually their extended-family members. Sometimes certain family members do not receive this news very well. It means that changes are going to take place, and sometimes change is not welcome.

But even if the news isn't received well, it doesn't change the fact of the pregnancy. It does mean, however, that some adjustments of attitudes will need to take place. When a family realizes they are pregnant it is not time for the birth. God has wisely given nine months for everyone to prepare for the birth of the baby.

When a church is pregnant with a vision it is not time for the birth. There is a maturing of the pregnancy so that a healthy birth takes place, in the fullness of time

The Heads of Ministries

During the first few months of pregnancy, it remains, for the most part, unnoticed. However, the time comes when everyone knows about the pregnancy. If a couple does announce that they are expecting a baby, they usually first tell their closest friends (after having told their family). The heads of ministries in the local church would represent that level of relationships. Your close friends should know about the pregnancy before it becomes public knowledge. Since family and friends now know about the pregnancy, they become a support system for the months ahead.

In the church this support system is the elders and the heads of ministries. As the church moves towards the birth of the vision, the event is covered in prayer. The elders and the pastor of the church have a support system in place for the birth of the vision.

The Whole Church

Finally, there comes a time when everyone is told about the expected arrival of a baby. Likewise, the entire church is brought into the birth process of the vision for that church. As the due date approaches and the birth is imminent, the whole body eagerly awaits the day of birth.

Birth Is the Beginning

Finally, the day arrives and the new baby is born. It is a day of great rejoicing. However, that is the day we also realize that giving birth is not the end of the process, but rather is only the beginning. Likewise concerning birthing a vision in the church, it is going to require walking, embracing, nurturing, and maturing in order for the vision to become viable and fruitful. Just as we walk with, embrace, and nurture a child to maturity, so it is with the vision of the local church. The birth is only the beginning; the real work lies ahead and will only be realized as we commit to the maturing process.

God's Vision, God's Provision

It is good to realize that the vision of God is not without His provision. Provision is what God supplies in order for the vision to bring success to the church and glory to Him. The vision of God carries within it certain characteristics that cause the local church to be blessed as they fulfill His vision.

Victory

The vision of God is the road to victory. His vision will bring us to our destiny with victory in our hearts. When we are following His vision, no weapon formed against us will prosper. We will, with each new revelation, become the evidence of God's victory in every community where He has established His church, the fullness of Him in the face of the earth.

Stability

God's vision brings every congregation to a place of stability. When something is stable, it is firmly established. Someone who is stable is one who is emotionally and mentally healthy. That is what God's vision brings to the local church. A local church with vision will be steady in purpose, constant, and consistent, unwavering in its quest to fulfill God's purpose in the community where it is established.

Peace

God's vision brings peace to the house. A place of peace is a place of rest and recovery. It is also a place where hearing becomes easier because there is no distracting noise or confusion to use up our energy and time. When there is an absence of peace, our being grows weary as it longs for that place of harmony and security. Our most productive living is experienced in an environment of peace.

Focus

Vision and focus are uniquely related. Focus is the point where the eyes adjust to bring forth a clear image. If there is not vision, there is no need to focus. Without focus there is no clear direction. Without clear direction we wander aimlessly. The local church needs to be able to focus on what they are and why they are there. This is only possible when a viable vision is in place. A corporate focus fosters unity in the church. When we are all focused on the same vision, only then are we all looking in the same direction. "Where brethren dwell together in unity, God commands the blessing."

Progress

Every congregation realizes a sense of success and fulfillment when there is progress. One of the most undesirable and discouraging places people can find themselves is in a place lacking progress. "Why are we doing this? We never seem to get anywhere. It's always the same old thing. How many times do we have to go around this mountain?" A lack of progress fosters discontentment, resentment, and rebellion.

To the Church

What an exciting prospect it is for us to be part of the birth of the vision for the local church. We have the responsibility to bring forth a successful birth.

When the body rejects the pregnancy it is called "spontaneous abortion." Too many times that is the experience in the local church. Instead of a healthy birth they have an abortion. After an abortion there is a barren womb. All too often this is the condition of the church, an aborted birth and an empty womb. Sometimes the abortion is so painful that the idea of entertaining another birth is more than leadership can endure, and so we live in this state of progressive blindness rather than vision. How tragic for the local church to be found in this condition.

When leadership announces we are pregnant with vision, it is our responsibility to bring forth a healthy birth to that vision.

CHAPTER EIGHT

The Structure of the Local Church

> Now you are the body of Christ, and members individually.
> And God has appointed these in the church: first apostles, second prophets, third teachers.
> 1 Corinthians 12:27-28

> Be shepherds of God's flock that is under your care, serving as overseers - not because you must, but because you are willing, as God wants you to be; not greedy for money, but eager to serve.
> 1 Peter 5:2 NIV

The church in the United States has suffered dramatically because it often refuses to embrace its leaders as God's sovereign choice to govern the church. God raises up leaders, the church does not. The church's responsibility is to embrace and prove the leaders whom God raises up.

Viable Church Leaders

How many sermons have we preached using the illustration of a slightly polluted glass of water, asking the question, "Would you like to drink from this glass? It is almost pure; it is only slightly polluted." The point being, no one willingly drinks from such a glass of water. Unfortunately, many times we church leaders ask people to embrace leadership that is slightly less than acceptable. Leadership in the church needs to be selected using the biblical approach seen in 1st and 2nd Timothy and Titus.

Leadership needs to be developed and proven through the dynamics of the "School of the Apostles." (This is a term I have adopted to describe the training process Jesus used in the preparation of the apostles.) We have a tendency to embrace a long-distance leadership development plan rather than the one Jesus modeled for us. He chose to relate closely to the individuals He was preparing for leadership in the church. Emerging leaders need to be brought alongside proven leaders to be mentored as leaders in the church.

What I am saying is not new; I'm sure that you have considered the importance of emerging leaders being connected to proven leaders who are honorable in the local church. However, my experience has been that this very basic need does not receive the priority it deserves.

I also want to challenge us in the area of presenting a viable local church structure that brings peace and security rather than vulnerability and unrest.

A Divine Appointment

Over the years, encountering divine appointments has been a great blessing to me. There have been times when I have separated myself from the busyness of the day to seek His face. Other times God breaks in on my day when I least expect Him. Divine appointments have radically changed my perspective and direction.

The doctor's office is not high on my list of favorite places to visit. Generally when I go it is because I have a condition that needs to be remedied. I am looking for information to find healing of some kind. On one occasion I found myself in the waiting room of the chiropractor. While waiting for my appointment, I busied myself with the various pieces of literature and magazines on the table. As I looked around at the plaques and diplomas on the walls, my eyes rested on a large poster that displayed in detail the skeleton of the human body, highlighting the spinal column. The chiropractor's office was an appropriate place to have this cleverly designed poster, since it causes you to focus on the spinal column. As I studied the poster, my eyes came to the words written across the bottom: "Structure Determines Function." The words not only stuck in my mind, they also stuck in my spirit: *Structure determines function!*

The divine appointment that I was to keep that day was not the one I had arranged with the doctor, although it was very helpful to my physical well-being. It was the one God arranged for me in the waiting room. He began to speak to me about the need for the body of Christ to have structure. He used the poster as an analogy for the structure of the local church.

Structure

I would like to take the mystery out of the word "structure" by looking at the definition offered in Webster's Dictionary.

- Something built (as a house or a dam); also: something made up of interdependent parts in a definite pattern of organization

- Arrangement or relationship of elements (as particles, parts, or organs) in a substance, body, or system

God designed the church with structure, and He tells us in Psalm 127:1 the builder is the Lord.

> Unless the LORD builds the house, they labor
> in vain who build it.
>
> Psalms 127:1

When it comes to local church structure there is an army of critics. Many of their criticisms are justified, because of the people involved, not because of the Master Builder. The design of the Master Builder is perfect, but the structure, because of the weakness of man's flesh, falters at times.

I find it interesting that Paul relates the body of Christ to the human body so that we might gain understanding from his analogy. Perhaps this is why the Lord used that diagram of the human skeleton to bring revelation and understanding to me.

Let's examine the analogy further. Try to imagine a human body without structure, having no arrangement or relationship among its various elements. It would be a large, formless blob! Can you imagine yourself without structure?

Suppose you were a large blob, with no structure, and someone asked you to move from one place to another. What a gross sight you would be, trying to move the blob with no success, your unorganized parts working against one another, trying to accomplish something they can only accomplish together. Truly, **structure determines function.**

The sight is equally gross when we find a local church body trying to function without a structure, with each of its unorganized parts working against itself. The truth of the statement on the poster applies to the body of Christ: **"Structure Determines Function."** That is why God has designed the church with structure. It is impossible for the church to accomplish her purpose without structure.

God's Design

The Skeletal Frame

One of the key elements in the structure of the body is the skeleton. That was the main point of the poster. Consider the purpose of the body's skeletal frame. It is to provide support, with joints that function as hinges on which every action of the body turns.

The leaders in the body of Christ serve the same purpose in the church as the skeleton does in the physical body. They are the support on which every action hinges. In reality, it is the body in cooperation with the structure that gives it the ability to move. The same is true in the church. It is the body of believers cooperating with their leaders that produces the desired result.

Without structure the body will not move progressively. The structure, though unseen, gives definition to its shape and function. The local church, by God's design, has leaders set in place in an organized manner, providing support, bearing the burden of movement, and bringing definition to the local church.

The Backbone of the Church

The backbone on the poster was highlighted, identifying its importance in the overall structure. The pastor and the elders (the presiding elder or deacons, depending on how you name those key leaders in the local church) are the backbone of the structure that is visible in the church.

The backbone, in the physical sense, is the channel for the nervous system, the means by which the head communicates with every part of the body. Not a single nerve goes directly to any part of the body without first going through the backbone. Every action results from the communication that takes place through the nervous system. That communication flows through the channel of the backbone and is distributed to each part of the body. The parts of the body that respond appropriately begin to move and function to accomplish the desire of the head of the body.

The local church body is designed with leaders who bear the burden of uninterrupted clear communication from the Head to the local church.

The Backbone Bears the Weight

In addition the backbone bears the weight of the whole body. When I am traveling in Uganda and Kenya it is common to see women walking along the road with very large, heavy loads upon their heads. This is strange to my eyes because in the United States that would not be common.

However, it is my understanding that this is the best way for the human body to carry a heavy load. When the load is on the head, the backbone bears the weight, distributing it throughout the body. It is interesting that the different parts of the body bear different degrees of the load, however, each part of the body is required to participate in order for the load to be carried successfully. When I see an African woman carrying a heavy load I don't conclude that her backbone is carrying the load; I conclude that her body is carrying the load.

It is the pastor and the elders in the local church who bear the weight of the body. They distribute the burden of that weight to different parts of the body in such a manner as to involve the whole body in the process of walking out what God has called the local church to accomplish.

Impairing the Structure

Backbone Injury

If the backbone is injured in any way, the function of the body is altered, even to the point of becoming paralyzed (dysfunctional). The backbone of the local church becomes one of the key areas for the focus of Jezebelic attack. If the role of the backbone (eldership) is wounded in any way by Jezebelic activity, then the attack takes its toll by impairing their function and the body suffers, even to the point of being dysfunctional (paralyzed).

Broken Bones

Since the entire skeletal frame is important for the functioning of the body, any injury to any part of the frame impedes its function. The overseers of ministries in the church make up the skeletal frame of the spiritual body. They serve by supporting the various functions of the local church vision.

This is the reason these areas in the body are a primary focus of attack by the Jezebel spirit. Causing harm to the leaders and the overseers of ministries will result in the body being unable to function properly. The assignment of the Jezebel spirit is to stop the purposes of God. The enemy of our soul knows that if the structure is damaged or destroyed, the function of the church is also damaged or destroyed.

The Rest of the Body

The backbone and the skeletal frame are key areas of attack, but it does not stop there. In the physical body when one member is hurting, it has the attention of the whole body. When your project requires the use of a hammer and you hit the wrong nail, the body not only knows instant pain, but the completion of the project is delayed.

If this scenario is repeated over and over again, the project not only is delayed it may never be completed. Likewise, the Jezebelic attack is equally effective as members of the body of Christ experience injury. The attack is designed to hinder or stop the purposes of God in a local church.

The Church Structure

The Structure and Benefits Are Not Beyond Our Grasp

Once again I am going to touch on a subject that cannot be exhausted in the context of this book. Entire books have been, and will continue to be, written on this subject. However, I think it is necessary to take the time to look briefly at what God has set as the structure and authority in the church. This is a significant topic if we are going to succeed in this battle of overcoming the Jezebel spirit.

God set in place all that is needed for the church to be successful, and the design He has chosen, when embraced, will not only succeed but will bring glory to Him in the church.

We get ourselves into trouble when we read something in Scripture and then take a position that it is impossible for us to understand; we settle for life without wisdom and revelation.

I am not discounting study and discussion, which help each of us draw conclusions regarding our personal theology. Nor am I discounting colleges and universities that offer courses on Bible and Christian Theology. All of these are useful for the purposes of God.

However, I challenge the belief that the truths spoken of in Scripture are beyond the ability of the average person to embrace. This is just simply not true. The benefits of structure and authority in the church are not beyond the grasp of the understanding of the most common intellect.

His Church

The church is made up of people who believe in Jesus, the Christ; they are identified together as the body of Christ, the household or family of God, the people of God. All of these terms are used to describe the representation of God's fullness in the earth, His church. (See Ephesians 1:22-23.)

> But now God has set the members, each one of them, in the body just as He pleased. And if they were all one member, where would the body be? But now indeed there are many members, yet one body.
>
> 1 Corinthians 12:18-20

God Has Designed the Church Structure With Three Elements

When Paul greets the Church at Philippi, he reveals specific elements, which make up the church.

> Paul and Timothy, servants of Jesus Christ, to all the saints in Christ Jesus who are in Philippi, with the bishops and deacons.
>
> Philippians 1:1

The elements that are revealed are "the ministry gifts" (Paul and Timothy), "the people" (the saints), and "the leaders" (bishops *(overseers)* and the deacons). We see clearly through this passage, the three elements of God's design for the structure of the church. Each element of God's design is set in place with specific ministry responsibilities, so the church can be victorious as we fulfill the purposes of God.

It is necessary for us to recognize the difference between the structure and the function of the church. The ministries to which we are called are the function of the church. The place from which we function is the structure.

Christians are unique in that everybody who identifies with the church, by the grace of God, has been called to a place of ministry. We should all function in the call that God has on our lives, committing back to Him our talents and the resources that He has given us stewardship over. In order for the church to succeed, God has given specific ministries, with unique identities and functions, so that we might work and live together in harmony and unity to accomplish His purposes and bring glory to Him.

1. The People in the Church

The first element to be recognized, are the saints, the people of the church. This is the simplest of truths as we look at the structure of the church. The church, by the grace of God, consists of the individuals who, by faith, have received salvation through accepting what Christ accomplished for them through His death on the cross.. The church is a wonderful blend of people with unique distinctives that have developed because of location, mission, call, and philosophy.

The people in the church are clearly the most significant element in the over-all identity of the church, His body. He intends to use all of us to represent His fullness in the earth.

2. The Church Leaders

The second element of the structure consists of the leaders in the church and these leaders function in three areas.

a. Heads of Ministries

These individuals are the church leaders who have answered God's call to serve as overseers of specific areas of ministry. We often find them networking with others as they seek to fulfill the call of God on their lives. Every area of ministry in the local church should be nurtured and cared for by people who are motivated by the passion and call they have for that specific area of ministry.

These individuals have been recognized and set in place by the overseers of the local church (the elders) to accomplish the vision and purpose of that church. They are people who are under the authority of the elders, and they function in their role of leadership with authority and accountability.

There have been people who are overseeing an area of ministry drawn into Jezebelic activity because they assume roles that are the responsibility of the elders in the church. The enemy of our souls loves this dilemma.

b. The Elders

This area of leadership is crucial for the safety and security of the church. However, we have so politicized this call on individuals' lives that the integrity of the ministry of elder is often compromised.

The specific purpose and function of recognized elders is spiritual oversight and care. These individuals are called of God and are set in place by apostolic ministry, who recognize the call as an elder on their lives.

Let us consider two areas of Scripture to help bring clarity to the function of elders. The first is Paul's letter to Timothy concerning elders. In his letter he speaks often of their function.

> Let the elders who rule well be counted worthy
> of double honor, especially those who labor in
> the word and doctrine.
>
> 1 Timothy 5:17

The word "rule" in this verse is translated from the Greek word *proistemi,* (pro-is'-tay-mee): to stand before, i.e. (in rank) to preside, or (by implication.) to practice: maintain, be over, rule. It is obvious that elders have a place of God-given authority in the church that is uniquely different from others.

The second reference is made as Peter speaks an exhortation to the elders, also mentioning their function.

> The elders who are among you I exhort, I who am a fellow elder and a witness of the sufferings of Christ, and also a partaker of the glory that will be revealed: Shepherd the flock of God which is among you, serving as overseers, not by compulsion but willingly, not for dishonest gain but eagerly;
>
> 1Peter 5:1-2

In this passage we find words revealing the function of elders. In verse two the word "shepherd" is translated from the Greek word *poimaino* (poy-mah'ee-no): to tend as a shepherd (or figuratively, supervisor); feed (cattle), rule.

Also in verse two the word "overseer" is translated from the Greek word *episkopeo* (ep-ee-skop-eh'-o): to oversee; by implication, to beware: -look diligently, take the oversight.

Elders are charged with the responsibility to tend God's people as a shepherd and to diligently take oversight and care. We can see by the function and purpose of the ministry of elders how significant their role is to the health and well-being of the church. They are extremely important as a functioning part of the structure of the church.

c. The Deacons

To see clearly the structure of the church it is necessary for us to look at this crucial area of ministry. Deacons carry the very important responsibility of serving the daily, practical needs of the church. We have two areas of Scripture for reference to understand their function and purpose.

> Likewise deacons must be reverent, not double-tongued, not given to much wine, not greedy for

money, holding the mystery of the faith with a pure conscience. But let these also first be proved; then let them serve as deacons, being found blameless. Likewise their wives must be reverent, not slanderers, temperate, faithful in all things. Let deacons be the husbands of one wife, ruling their children and their own houses well. For those who have served well as deacons obtain for themselves a good standing and great boldness in the faith which is in Christ Jesus.

1TI 3:8 - 13

In this passages the word "deacon" is translated from the Greek word *diakonos* (dee-ak'-on-os); probably from an obscure word *diako* (to run on errands; an attendant), i.e. (generally) a waiter (at table or in other menial duties); specifically, a Christian teacher and pastor (technically a deacon or deaconess): deacon, minister, servant. This clearly identifies their role and function in the church.

Traditionally scholars have looked at the following passage in the book of Acts as the initial appointing of deacons in the church. However, the difference between what is seen here and what we see in the previous two references is the use of the word deacon.

Then the twelve summoned the multitude of the disciples and said, "It is not desirable that we should leave the word of God and serve tables. Therefore, brethren, seek out from among you seven men of good reputation, full of the Holy Spirit and wisdom, whom we may appoint over this business; but we will give ourselves continually to prayer and to the ministry of the word."

Acts 6:2-4

Even though this passage does not contain the word deacon, we can recognize that the function outlined in the passage is in keeping with the definition of the Greek word *diakonos*. The word "serve" is translated from the Greek word *diakoneo,* which means to be an attendant, i.e. to wait upon as a host, friend, or teacher; to act as a deacon.

Thus, we can see why this passage is looked to for direction not only in understanding the function of deacons, but also how they are selected and set in place.

As with the role of elder, we can see how important the role of deacon is to the overall success of the structure of the church. They are servants, called to serve in specific ways to meet the needs of the local church, releasing the elders to function in their role in the church. Without them the ministry of the church is greatly hindered.

3. "The Ministry gifts," ("The Ascension Gifts," "The Fivefold Ministry Gifts")

This last element of the structure of the church is crucial to the success of the church fulfilling its commission. The ministry gifts in Ephesians 4:11 are given by God for the specific purpose of equipping and maturing. God in His infinite wisdom set in place ministry gifts to prepare the church to accomplish her mission.

Fivefold Ministry

> It was he who gave some to be apostles, some to be prophets, some to be evangelists, and some to be pastors and teachers.
>
> Ephesians 4:11 NIV

From within the church God gives ministry gifts that are extremely important for the success of the church, and the Scriptures are so clear about the need for these ministry gifts. It is incumbent upon each person to embrace the five-fold ministry gifts for the successful maturing and ministry of the church. The value of these ministry gifts is seen clearly in Ephesians 4:12-15:

> for the equipping of the saints for the work of ministry, for the edifying of the body of Christ, till we all come to the unity of the faith and of the knowledge of the Son of God, to a perfect man, to the measure of the stature of the fullness of Christ; that we should no longer be children, tossed to and fro and carried about with every wind of doctrine, by the trickery of men, in the cunning craftiness of deceitful plotting, but, speaking the truth in love, may grow up in all things into Him who is the head – Christ.
>
> Ephesians 4:12-15

Additionally, I want to clearly state that though some of the fivefold ministry gifts function outside of the local church, they remain a strategic part of the leadership within the local church. Ideally each church has a pastor, and each pastor is in relationship with apostolic ministry, as well as prophetic, evangelistic, and teaching ministry.

Without the ascension gifts the church would be ill equipped to accomplish her mission and purpose. We must see the ascension gifts functioning effectively in the church. The Jezebelic attack is designed by the enemy of God to destroy the effectiveness of these ministry gifts.

Concerning the Authority

Each ministry gift has a God-given authority, which is unique to and for that ministry gift. The authority of one ministry is different from the others, and each one's authority is uniquely germane to the ministry gift.

God-given authority of these gifts, like all God-given authority in the church (i.e. elders, deacons, heads of ministries) can only function in spheres of influence developed through relationships. These relationships must be based on the foundation of love.

If the authority given to and for ministry is exercised void of relationship based on love, it becomes a religious, legalistic, "lording-over" kind of authority. This is not God's intention.

We miss the fullness of God's provision for His church if we do not embrace all the gifts He has given to equip the church for the work of ministry.

Local Church Government

The topics of church structure and government are very important and we cannot do them justice by discussing them as a brief part of this book. However, it is important for us to consider the structure of the body and the philosophy of church government to successfully deal with Jezebelic activity.

The Philosophy

I realize my comments in this area will cause some to rejoice, some to be challenged, and others to reject what I have to offer. Sometimes our position on these issues is cast in stone by history and tradition. My comments are not to find fault with what some have chosen as the philosophy of church government, but rather to express what seems to be apparent to me as the method the apostles used to establish local churches.

When considering the philosophy of church government, it is necessary to understand that the leadership of the local church is more than a body of organized leaders. The leadership of the local church is made up of God-ordained leaders, empowered with authority in order to govern the body of believers.

We should not shy away from the words "authority" and "govern." They have been part of the function of God's leaders throughout the history of the church as witnessed in the Old and New Testaments. Even from the time of Adam and Eve, the instruction from God was that they were to "rule over" the earth *(Genesis 1:28)*. This indicates that a measure of authority was given to them.

There are reasons why people object to church leaders having this place of authority. The church has experienced the abuse of power and authority when the actions of men are motivated by desires of the flesh. Remember, the seedbed for destruction is the flesh of man.

The Democratic Philosophy

Americans have found that a government "of the people, by the people, and for the people" is the best approach to living in peace and harmony. Because of the success we have enjoyed in our secular society, we have brought the same process into the church. Democracy as a form of government for the church is not found in Scripture. I might also add that this philosophy is not seen in other countries. It seems to be primarily a western worldview of church government.

Politics and Church Government

The secular democratic philosophy of a government of the people, by the people, for the people, requires the dynamics of politics to succeed. People are politically successful when they have won favor by gaining emotional and intellectual approval of the majority of people involved in a society.

The political process embraces whatever means is necessary to gain this approval. What happens in the secular social realm of a democratic society is the flawed reasoning that whatever it takes to win the majority is acceptable, because the end result justifies the means. Sometimes this governmental process suffers because of the unspoken, unacceptable means that are used by politicians whose personal desires are below the moral or ethical standard of the society they are trying to influence.

The end result is a corrupt government, not because of the individuals in the governing process as a whole, but because of corrupt individuals in the government that affect the whole society.

Destined to Fail in the Church

When a church embraces the philosophy of a democratic government, the philosophy requires the same political dynamics as a secular society.

The dichotomy is this: the "majority rule" governing process can be accomplished by a political process as well as by the Spirit. From a puritanical sense we would hope that the majority rule would be as a result of a leading of the Holy Spirit. However, this has not been our experience. It has always been the downfall of man to implement, by personal influence, what God means to accomplish by His Spirit.

Just as in the secular democratic society, the church has individuals who enter into a political process using unacceptable means to accomplish their own personal desires. They even embrace the philosophy that the end justifies the means. The results are the same as the secular society: a corrupt government.

The church sets itself up to fail when we embrace the democratic philosophy as a governing process because the seedbed of destruction by Jezebelic activity is the flesh. The democratic philosophy requires a political process which is motivated by the flesh more often than by the Holy Spirit. This becomes a chink in the armor.

Paul expresses this weakness of the flesh so well in Romans Chapter Eight.

> There is therefore now no condemnation to those who are in Christ Jesus, who do not walk according to the flesh, but according to the Spirit. For the law of the Spirit of life in Christ Jesus has made me free from the law of sin and death. For what the law could not do in that it was weak through the flesh, God did by sending His own Son in the likeness of sinful flesh, on account of sin: He condemned sin in the flesh, that the righteous requirement of the law might be fulfilled in us who do not walk according to the flesh but according to the Spirit.
>
> Romans 8:1-4

> So then, those who are in the flesh cannot please God.
>
> Romans 8:8

The political process embraces the activity of the flesh that is required to win favor emotionally and intellectually to establish a democratic form of government.

An Illusion of Who Is in Charge

A democratic form of church government creates and gives the illusion that the congregation is in charge in the church. When we believe that illusion, then the One who is in charge is routinely ignored for the sake of what the majority perceive is best for the church.

This philosophy of government creates an environment that fosters the dynamics of politics in the church. Governing through a political process reduces the standard for quality leadership and is only dependant on one's ability to succeed politically.

Circumventing God's Design and Desire

It also violates the ordained structure of God's leaders to govern with authority. When we create a government of the people, by the people, and for the people, then the people circumvent God's sovereign choice for oversight. This is not God's design or His desire. If the church is truly established in His kingdom, then we must embrace His philosophy for church government.

Some would say this is impossible for us to do, and they would be correct if indeed we do it in and of ourselves. We should heed Paul's admonition to the Galatians:

> Are you so foolish? Having begun in the Spirit, are you now being made perfect by the flesh?
> Galatians 3:3

Of course he is talking about Jewish law, but the principle remains the same: it is foolish to depend on the flesh for what God has started in the spirit.

Successfully Defeating the Jezebelic Attack

As I pointed out, this subject cannot be fully discussed in just a few paragraphs. My goal was not to give an exhaustive commentary, but rather to identify the structure and authority as being biblically valid and necessary.

We are ill-equipped to defeat a Jezebelic attack if we have not made every effort to implement God's design of biblical structure and authority and establish it in the church. He has designed His church to be overcomers.

CHAPTER NINE

Stopping the Jezebelic Attack

> Let this mind be in you which was also in Christ
> Jesus, who, being in the form of God, did not
> consider it robbery to be equal with God, but
> made Himself of no reputation, taking the form
> of a bondservant, and coming in the likeness of
> men. And being found in appearance as a man,
> He humbled Himself and became obedient to
> the point of death, even the death of the cross.
>
> Philippians 2:5-8

In this chapter I want to discuss a very significant issue relative to stopping the attack of the Jezebel spirit. In Chapters Seven and Eight I discussed in depth the importance of the vision and structure of the church relative to stopping Jezebelic activity. These two elements must be in place if we are going to stop the attack of the Jezebel spirit. It is imperative for the leadership in the church to establish a vision and structure of integrity. The church cannot succeed unless this happens.

We challenge and condemn leaders who fail to establish a viable vision and structure in the church. But the truth is, I have seen leadership do an excellent job of establishing both yet still find themselves in the midst of turmoil in their local church, suffering from the attack of the Jezebel spirit.

A healthy spiritual environment is necessary in order for the vision and structure to accomplish all that God intends. The proper spiritual environment is dependent on the combination of several conditions; however, there is one principle that must be embraced to see the fruitfulness of the vision and structure of the local church. This key principle is the one demonstrated in the life of Jesus, which is His willingness to die to self. In Philippians 2:5-8 we see clearly a reference to two deaths. One is His death on the cross, and the other is humbling Himself, being obedient to the point of death (which in our lives can be interpreted as dying to self).

Die to Self

The truth is that we cannot prevent the attack of the Jezebel spirit. However, we can stop the attack and alter the outcome. In order for us to stop the attack and to minimize the effect of Jezebelic activity, we must embrace His Kingdom and its principles. When the structure and vision is in place, there yet remains a crucial element that must be resident within us. There must be a willingness to die to self if we are going to stop the attack of the Jezebel spirit.

Every individual in the church, including each leader, finds stability and security in the vision and structure of the church. Yet they can only experience that stability and security when each dies to self. We all have our own opinions and personal desires. However, a properly established vision and structure represents the will of God for a local congregation. When we choose not to die to self, we are not submitting to what God has established in the church.

In order for a Jezabelic attack to be successful, it must have a means to become viable in the church. As we have pointed out, the flesh (carnal nature) of man is the place where the seeds of destruction are planted. Those seeds will not be able to germinate if there is a willingness to die to self.

Wrapped Up in Self

The attack of the Jezebel spirit will manifest itself and be successful when the one it is using to accomplish its mission is wrapped up in self. Since manipulation and control are a major part of the Jezebel spirit's modus operandi, someone who is wrapped up in self is extremely vulnerable to be used in the attack.

When an individual's reference for all life experience must be processed through a heart that is dedicated to self, then all responses are limited to that which fulfills self, that which serves self, for instance:

> self-centered, self-promoting, self-focused, self-righteous, self-absorbed, self-acting, self-adjusting, self-advancement, self-aggrandizing, self-appointed, self-assertive, self-conceit, self-concern, self-condemned, self-confident, self-congratulatory, self-constituted, self-created, self-deception, self-definition, self-delusion, self-despair, self-determination, self-esteem, self-explaining, self-governing, self-identity, self-importance, self-induced, self-indulgent, self-interest, self-perception, self-perpetuating, self-pity, self-preservation, self-proclaimed, self-protection, self-referential, self-regard, self-reliant, self-revelation, self-rule, self-satis-fied, self-sustaining, and self-taught.

When we read through this list of self-centered activities, it is easy to see how one can be drawn into control and manipulation. Dying to self moves us into a safe place, a place where the Jezebel spirit has no foothold.

A Struggle for Peace and Well-Being

Being wrapped up in self is a result of our struggle for peace and well-being. I believe everyone's decision to become a member of a local church is based on his or her sense of peace and well-being. People who do not have that sense will be a contributing factor to the erosion of the stability of the local church. When people begin to verbalize and demonstrate their discontent, the seeds of destruction planted in our flesh have a place to germinate and bear fruit.

Flesh Struggles for Survival

Our flesh struggles for survival, and key to that survival is the peace and well-being of self. We process the vision and our relationship to the structure of the local church by evaluating how it affects us. If we are ill at ease, our sense of peace and well-being is jeopardized. We begin to look for avenues and opportunities for self-preservation. When this happens, our actions can be motivated out of our struggle to gain or regain a sense of peace and well-being. All of our actions and relationships will bear the same condemning characteristic of being self-centered.

A person who is self-centered and self-indulgent soon takes on the identity of being motivated out of selfish ambitions. Dying to self becomes more and more difficult and eventually impossible without true repentance and a renewing of the mind.

Choosing Peace and Well-Being

Generally, our response when asked, "How are you doing?" is based on how we feel. How we feel is based on a sense of peace and well-being. Peace and well-being have to do with our current state, relative to the past and future. Sometimes, our history and our future hold us in bondage when we consider our well-being.

Our past can push us into a sense of guilt and remorse. When that happens our only escape is to alter the source of the guilt or remorse. Since history is what it is and cannot be altered, we are cast into a sea of hopelessness. We can also be held hostage by our future. Knowing the details, or maybe not knowing the details, of our destiny can cause us to live in fear and apprehension. Both our past and our future can rob us of our security, and that puts us in a place of unrest. The result is that we are living without a sense of peace.

A desire for peace and well-being is inherent with humanity. Every human being has a base survival need to see peace established in his or her life. Based on that need we are dedicated to the pursuit of peace and well-being in our personal lives. The challenge is to embrace the process that brings us to that place of peace.

> Peace I leave with you, My peace I give to you; not as the world gives do I give to you. Let not your heart be troubled, neither let it be afraid.
>
> John 14:27

In this passage we see clearly how the peace Jesus gives is uniquely different from the peace we have and can receive from the world. However, there is a process to receiving the peace that He gives. The process is dying to self.

Peace Outside His Kingdom Is Temporal

When we consider our past, the life we lived outside the kingdom of God, it is obvious any peace that exists is temporal. In reality we have peace as long as things are going well for us. We know that things do not always go well. Many of life's dealings are responsible for the demise of our peace. There is, however, a peace that comes from God. His peace is a peace that not only overshadows unrest but also is the foundation for our moving through difficult times. The only way for a person to receive His peace is by dying to self and receiving the gift of God, which is eternal life through the death His Son died on the cross.

When we receive Jesus and confess our sins (those sins of our past that carry consequences, one of which is unrest: a lack of peace and well being), we have the assurance from a faithful God that He will forgive our sins and make them as though they never were.

When we do not have the promise and guarantee of eternal life, we do not have peace because of the uncertainty of our eternal destiny. When we die to self and receive His salvation through Christ's redemptive work on the cross, having come to the knowledge of His Kingdom for our daily lives, we are filled with an overwhelming eternal peace. This peace goes beyond any circumstance of our past, present, and future. This peace is a fruit of our knowing God, Who has in mind for us a future with a hope.

> For I know the thoughts that I think toward you, says the LORD, thoughts of peace and not of evil, to give you a future and a hope.
> Jeremiah 29:11

What is the key element to the process of securing peace and well-being? Dying to self.

> Then Jesus said to His disciples, "If anyone desires to come after Me, let him deny himself, and take up his cross, and follow Me."
> Matthew 16:24

Choosing Peace in the Church

Let us break in on Sam's "self talk" (thoughts). He is about to make wrong choices based on his self-centered perspective:

"This is the third time I've talked to Pastor Al about the worship team. He just doesn't get it! The service is much too long. It actually goes past 12:00. He knows that little league starts at 2:00, and there's just not enough time to eat and get to the field in time for warm ups. ... I offered to be on the worship team; I even offered to be the worship leader and he knows I could do it.... If I were the worship leader we would be done on time.... I know what I'll do; I'll take a poll of the families in the church with children in little league and see if they feel the same way I do. I'll bet I am not the only one who feels the service is too long.... I am convinced he does not even care about our family life. He seems so disconnected from us.... If I need to I will request a special meeting with the elders. He will find out who is in charge. He is kidding himself if he thinks he is in charge.... The elders will do the right thing. They know if they do not I will take this to the congregation. If the leadership can't get this straightened out, we will do it for them."

Who knows how this will go? The Jezebel spirit is looking for someone just like Sam.

Actually, this scenario is not uncommon in churches where people decide on the length, breadth, and scope of ministry in the church based on how it affects them.

Here we have an individual who is not happy with how the worship service is affecting his ideal life. He has decided to change the situation. The one thing that is obvious is that the change must take place outside of his personal ambitions. This attitude reveals a lack of willingness on Sam's part to die to self (he has no peace).

He is willing to go to any length to force the changes he perceives as necessary to improve his quality of life. When people begin to move in the flesh, with selfish motives, the potential for them to be used by the Jezebel spirit is dramatically increased.

It is necessary for us to be ambassadors of peace, to live in peace, and be instruments of peace. The only way for that to happen is for us to die to self and embrace the vision and structure of the church. We need to elect peace as it pertains to self. The only way for this to happen is for us to set aside any motivation that is rooted in self.

Releasing the Potential Blessing

Dying to self releases the potential benefit and blessing of the structure and vision of a local church. This is a difficult thing to do but worth the effort, because it is the Kingdom principle which will bring about peace and well-being.

> Then I heard a loud voice saying in heaven, "Now salvation, and strength, and the kingdom of our God, and the power of His Christ have come, for the accuser of our brethren, who accused them before our God day and night, has been cast down. And they overcame him by the blood of the Lamb and by the word of their testimony, and they did not love their lives to the death. Therefore rejoice, O heavens, and you who dwell in them! Woe to the inhabitants of the earth and the sea! For the devil has come down to you, having great wrath, because he knows that he has a short time."
>
> Revelation 12:10-12

We cannot know this victory without dying to self and embracing His provision for our lives.

> Are you so foolish? After beginning with the Spirit, are you now trying to attain your goal by human [1] effort?
>
> Galatians 3:3 NIV

Let it not become our testimony that we take things into our own hands, trying to accomplish by our human effort what God means to accomplish by His design and plan, in order to establish His peace in our lives. We need to quickly embrace this principle of dying to self. It is impossible to know victory without dying to self and embracing His provision for our lives.

CHAPTER TEN

Defeating the Attack

Therefore, since we are receiving a kingdom that cannot be shaken, let us be thankful, and so worship God acceptably with reverence and awe, for our "God is a consuming fire."

Hebrews 12:28-29

A person's integrity is put in jeopardy when he or she becomes the focus of malicious gossip. Character assassination is an ongoing agenda of the Jezebel spirit. In Chapter Four I expressed at length the Jezebel spirit's strategy to destroy the integrity of leadership. I believe it is the same strategy the enemy uses on many individuals in the church. Destroying reputations is the strategy the enemy uses to bring into question godly character.

When you are the focus of malicious gossip, your reputation is tarnished and you become suspect in your relationship to the church. You will be passed over when people are being asked to serve in the ministry of the church. This experience is devastating to our emotions and self-worth. Because of our human nature, there is no way to escape the pain and distress of having your reputation maliciously maligned.

We know how difficult it is to overcome a bad reputation. Others will be influenced by what they hear until the truth has been revealed. Some will continue to be influenced negatively toward you even after the truth is revealed. The focus of this attack is to cause you to be dysfunctional in the church.

What Is Our Response?

Many times our response to an assassination attempt on our character is to try to save our reputation. This response has no effect on the real issue in defeating the attack. The real issue is character, not reputation. I am not suggesting that we not confront the Jezebelic activity and the unfounded accusations. I think it is necessary to confront it (see Chapter Fifteen) in order to minimize collateral damage from the attack. Many people will be affected by the character assassination attempt. Confronting the activity does not in itself defeat the Jezebelic attack or bring victory.

Our focus is to victoriously defeat the attack of the Jezebel spirit. No matter how severe the attack on our reputation, it does not affect our character. By destroying our reputation it only gives the appearance that our character is questionable. The attack does not destroy character; however, it can and does reveal character. The question is, what kind of character will be revealed? Godly character is above reproach. If we are to be victorious in this warfare, we must pursue godly character.

The Tongue Unbridled

Gossip, slander, and malicious talk are the hallmarks of the attack of the Jezebel spirit. It seems the most useful tool for this purpose is the tongue, when it is directed by the flesh of someone who is being used by the Jezebel spirit. This is a planned, precise launching of attack after attack in an effort to destroy the reputation and credibility of an individual, attempting to cause them to become ineffective in their pursuit of the will of God and His purposes.

> And the tongue is a fire, a world of iniquity. The tongue is so set among our members that it defiles the whole body, and sets on fire the course of nature; and it is set on fire by hell.
>
> James 3:6

The only thing that can stop the raging fire set by gossip is godly character. Godly character is something to be developed, embraced, and maintained.

Godly Character Is Fireproof

Character that is shaped by God is fireproof because it has been established by another fire, His consuming fire. Godly character can and will withstand the test of malicious attacks, because it is fireproof.

> According to the grace of God which was given to me, as a wise master builder I have laid the foundation, and another builds on it. But let each one take heed how he builds on it. For no other foundation can anyone lay than that which is laid, which is Jesus Christ. Now if anyone builds on this foundation with gold, silver, precious stones, wood, hay, straw, each one's work will become clear; for the Day will declare it, because it will be revealed by fire; and the fire will test each one's work, of what sort it is. If anyone's work which he has built on it endures, he will receive a reward. If anyone's work is burned, he will suffer loss; but he himself will be saved, yet so as through fire.
>
> 1 Corinthians 3:10-15

This passage cautions us to take heed how we build. The word heed in the original text is so rich in meaning; it is the word *blepo:* blep'-o; a prim. verb; to look at (literally or figuratively): behold, beware, lie, look , perceive, regard, see, sight, take heed. The implication is that this is serious business, building on the foundation of Jesus Christ. Some have expressed that Paul is addressing potential leaders in the church, perhaps ministries and ministers. However, I believe it would not violate the intent and spirit of the Scriptures to apply this passage to the building of godly character as well. Godly character is a necessity in the life of each believer who is going to be used to accomplish His purposes.

I do believe our character is destined to experience the test. The test of dealing with the destruction of our reputation is a very real test of godly character. May we not be found wanting when our character is revealed.

How Do We Build Godly Character?
It is God's grace and blessing for us to be able to have godly character. His design is for us to be changed into the likeness of His Son. There have been entire books written on this subject, however, I want to point out a very simple principle in building godly character. We must embrace godly character as the Holy Spirit reveals it to us. I believe this happens in two ways. The first is by reading and studying Scriptures that reveal to us the character and nature of Christ.

> All Scripture is given by inspiration of God, and is profitable for doctrine, for reproof, for correction, for instruction in righteousness, that the man of God may be complete, thoroughly equipped for every good work.

I charge you therefore before God and the
Lord Jesus Christ, who will judge the living and
the dead at His appearing and His kingdom.

2 Timothy 3:16 - 4:1

Too often this passage is viewed as a foundation and
license to adjust the character of others. I think the intent of
the passage is to challenge us to use the Scriptures for our
own reproof, correction, and instruction in righteousness.
God has given the Scriptures to build godly character.

The second is by the prompting of the Holy Spirit on a
moment-by-moment basis. In Isaiah 62 we see the commitment of God to relentlessly pursue His people in His quest
to bring them into His Godly character, or perhaps more
correctly stated, His bringing godly character into them.

For Zion's sake I will not keep silent, for
Jerusalem's sake I will not remain quiet, till her
righteousness shines out like the dawn, her
salvation like a blazing torch.

Isaiah 62:1 NIV

The words, "I will not keep silent," indicate He is speaking to them continuously. God is still speaking continuously
to His people. I am sure you have been in a situation where
you are confronted with a choice, and as you consider your
options the Holy Spirit begins to illuminate the godly
option. At that specific moment you have an opportunity to
embrace godly character or something less.

But the Helper, the Holy Spirit, whom the Father
will send in My name, He will teach you all
things, and bring to your remembrance all things
that I said to you.

John 14:26

Whether it is by the Holy Spirit's revelation through the Scriptures or by the Holy Spirit speaking to us directly, it is our embracing the revelation that builds godly character.

The Jezebel Spirit Is Defeated

The reason the Jezebel spirit is so concerned about our character is because of its potential to withstand the most devastating attempt to destroy our reputation. Keep in mind; the assignment of the Jezebel spirit is to destroy the purposes of God. When the battle lines are drawn and our enemy's arsenal is filled with those things that destroy reputation, proving the character of the one under attack is the anticipated result. What character will be revealed? This will be the deciding factor of who has the victory: the enemy of our soul or the one who is pursuing godly character. Godly character chooses the will of the Father Who desires His will be done on earth as it is in heaven.

When gossip has run its course with all its inflicted damage, godly character will still be standing to once again prove its integrity and trustworthiness.

The enemy of our soul wants to destroy or pervert godly character because that character is the only thing that will assure the recovery of an anointed, viable ministry, one that is called to accomplish God's purposes.

The call of God is without repentance on each individual's life. However, the call can be made ineffectual by the devastating attack of the Jezebel spirit. **God has provided a way for us not only to withstand the attack, but to defeat the enemy in the secure fortress of godly character as well.**

CHAPTER ELEVEN

Sheep Rustling

I urge you, brothers, to watch out for those who cause divisions and put obstacles in your way that are contrary to the teaching you have learned. Keep away from them. For such people are not serving our Lord Christ, but their own appetites. By smooth talk and flattery they deceive the minds of naive people.

Romans 16:17-18 NIV

Hanging up the phone, I sat and stared blankly at the wall in my office. My heart was filled with mixed emotions. I was angry and disappointed at the news I had just received. It was Bill, calling to assure me that he was not leaving the church. His heart was committed to this church and he would not be tempted to go anywhere.

When I asked what prompted this call of reassurance, I already knew the answer. Alice was continuing to carry out her plan to take as many people as she could with her, as she left the church. My mind was flooding with thoughts about the events that led up to this point.

She Carried Baggage

When they first came to the church, I was unduly influenced by what appeared to be a young couple having the very real potential to be a blessing to the church. They came with baggage (unresolved issues) from another local congregation. I was told they left that congregation when Alice was confronted about her actions and attitude. I met with Alice and her husband, George, to discuss the matter and felt that we had worked through the problems. They assured me that all was well with the leaders in the other church, and that their reason for leaving had nothing to do with the confrontation. When I spoke with the leaders in the other church, they confirmed what I was told by Alice and George.

There are two things I would like to say at this point regarding defeating the attack of the Jezebel spirit. One, we must work together, as leaders, when people come with unresolved issues. We need to be proactive in resolving these issues. Two, as leaders we must be honest with one another. I later heard that the leaders from the other church were glad to be rid of this couple and indicated that they left because she had been confronted. These leaders were disingenuous in their response to me. This was a missed opportunity to thwart an attack.

They let her go with unresolved issues, viewing it as the solution to their problem. Sometimes it cannot be helped; people leave churches when circumstances will not allow corrective ministry because of a loss of influence in their lives. However, in this case we were a neighboring church thinking we were opening the door for continued progress in resolving the issues. Unfortunately those leaders did not have enough concern for the church to become proactive in the process.

The result? Jezebelic activity that was active in one church now had the opportunity to continue in another. This should not be so. We must work together in order to prevent transference of the attack of the Jezebel spirit from one church to another.

Establishing Her Influence

As time went on it appeared that Alice knew something about everything that was going on, even if it wasn't her concern or responsibility. She had the ability to skillfully shape things around herself for her benefit.

Alice became very active in the church. She was ambitious and able to establish herself prominently in the life and ministry of the church. She involved herself in many areas and was effective in all of her endeavors to serve. She put herself forward on every occasion, successfully developing spheres of influence that she would exercise later.

It wasn't long before she began to approach me requesting to minister in specific ways that would place her in upfront and visible positions in the congregation. She began to gain prominence and influence among her peers and in the congregation. If she thought there was a possibility that her request would be denied, she enlisted others to approach me ahead of time, to tell me what a blessing they thought it would be if she had the opportunity to minister.

It was not long before the flesh that was out of control became very visible. She did not hesitate to deceive, and sometimes boldly lie, to give a right impression or get her way in specific given situations.

What Goes Around Comes Around

George, Alice's husband, was a gentle, loving man who could see no wrong in his wife. She was able to do and say harmful things right under his nose that he never recognized. Even though she gave the appearance of being submitted to her husband, she was not. She "ran the show" at home.

Finally the time came to begin the process of confrontation. First, it was with George; he needed to take control of his home and be the head of his household. Second, it was with Alice, to remove her from all active ministries in the church until the issues were resolved. This was more than she could bear, and so she once again began to plan an exit strategy. They announced they were moving from the area to be close to family, and they asked if they could stand before the congregation, announce what they were doing, and ask for prayer. I agreed to this only after they told me exactly what they were going to say. Their move would take them over a thousand miles away, so my only hope was that I would have the opportunity to dialogue with their new church leadership to continue the process.

Continuing to Deceive

I could not believe the events that took place after George and Alice stood before the congregation and announced their decision to leave the church and move out of state. We prayed for them and said goodbye. My concern for them was overshadowed by my concern for the congregation I pastored. I confess that I was glad to see them go; yet I still felt love and a sense of responsibility toward them.

Within days the sheep rustling began. In truth this couple did not leave the area. Rather, they started attending a new church in the area. It seems the pastor was not only embracing them but was also encouraging Alice to bring her friends. He desired to see his church grow.

The Jezebel Spirit Enlists Help

When I heard this, I called the pastor to discuss the issue; his response was one of suppressed delight. He just could not believe that I would be concerned because some of Alice's friends had joined her in this new church. He also couldn't understand why I would want to question people's choice to move on in God. After all, they were so excited about the fresh, new, anointed revelation they were receiving through his ministry of the Word. He saw no need to question her motives or challenge her for soliciting people from our congregation. This pastor was truly being used in Jezebelic activity, motivated by his own agenda.

> Remember what the Amalekites did to you along the way when you came out of Egypt. When **you were weary and worn out**, they met you on your journey and **cut off all who were lagging behind**; they had no fear of God.
>
> Deuteronomy 25:17-18 NIV

The Jezebelic Spirit Preys on the Vulnerable

Alice had selected her targets with skill, approaching those who were vulnerable to her influence. She picked those who were struggling in one way or another in their walk with the Lord. Promising them newfound peace and joy in this new church, she manipulated and seduced the weak and naïve based on their need. She picked people by appealing to their flesh, focusing on single adults and older teens. She committed herself to inciting a mass exodus from the church.

There are very few churches that do not experience sheep rustling in one form or another. Sheep rustling occurs when people are not willing to stand with the vision and structure of the church they attend. In this case, Alice was looking for those who were lagging behind. She was also looking for those who were disgruntled, who were in disagreement with something in the church. It could be the leadership or another church member. She selected people who had lost their passion for this particular church and its vision. These are the people who become vulnerable to the attack of the Jezebel spirit.

Every flock has stragglers; it is part of being a flock; stragglers are a reality. Some become so because of curiosity, checking out something new, unknown, or strange. For others it is due to a lack of interest; they appear complacent and apathetic in what the flock is doing. For still others it is lack of emotional and physical attachment. Sometimes people are weary and worn out, as we see in Deuteronomy 25:17-18, cut off and lagging behind. These people are vulnerable to the attack of the Jezebel spirit.

Sheepdogs

The shepherd's solution for keeping the stragglers safe is his ever-faithful sheepdogs. The sheepdog is an extension of the shepherd in the care and protection of the sheep. The sheepdog is under the direction of the shepherd and is committed to bring strays back into the fold. His role is a very active one, never resting, always pursuing the strays and stragglers, keeping them in a safe place.

Pastors, we need to have committed sheepdogs (visitation pastors) as we shepherd God's flock. We cannot change the existence of strays and stragglers, and we can't prevent the attack of the Jezebel spirit. However, we can provide for ongoing, active pursuit of those who appear to be straying and lagging behind. In the scripture referenced above, the Amalekites were picking off the stragglers and, as a result, some never reached the Promised Land. The same is true in our churches. The enemy of our souls will pick off the strays and stragglers, and some will never realize the promises of God in their lives.

A word to the sheep of the fold: you need to trust the love and care of the pastor God has given you. What a tragedy it is when a seasoned committed pastor's love, care, and protection becomes suspect simply because someone has presented what appears to be a better offer. **Church is not a candy store; it is a sheep shed. Stay put and be blessed!** Our life, which is hidden in Christ, has much more in store than your current perceived situation or circumstance. Perhaps there is a change coming in your life.

However, that change must be initiated by the Holy Spirit and then walked out with the counsel of the elders and pastor whom God has provided to care for your spiritual life. Do not fall prey to the Jezebelic activity of someone like Alice.

When do we realize the need to gather the strays? Often it is when it is too late, such as when we have an Alice that manifests Jezebelic activity by sheep rustling.

The end of the story is this: Alice and George did finally move from the area. The pastor of the new church asked them to leave, as they were a huge problem to him, trying to control the lives of people in the church. He even called to ask if I had any counsel to help him with this problem. The church closed after a brief start. The pastor, who was also a master of deception, was caught in the quagmire of his own actions, finding it impossible to continue in ministry.

What happened to the nine families who left our church to be a part of what they thought was a better church? Thankfully, some returned to be with us. Some joined other churches, feeling too embarrassed or uncomfortable to return, and still others might never know the fulfillment of the promises of God in their lives.

CHAPTER TWELVE

The Worship Team

Therefore, I urge you, brothers, in view of God's mercy, to offer your bodies as living sacrifices, holy and pleasing to God - this is your spiritual act of worship.

Romans 12:1

Silence fell in the room as the night's practice ended and the worship team left the platform. Another night of strife and disappointment; when will this end? The only sound heard were the heavy sighs coming from people, an expression of their disapproval, and the frustrated end of every effort they intended to make toward bringing peace to this ministry team. Ready to lead worship on Sunday? Hardly. Choosing to do it anyway? Absolutely.

Turmoil in the Team

Fred is the worship leader, but he is so insecure, he does not make the decisions that need to be made. Besides, even if he did, he would hear it from Sue who thinks she is helping through "leading by default" without the title or the authority. She's convinced she's "doing it for Jesus." Her biggest challenge right now is to convince the drummer that he is not the lead instrument. His problem results from being controlled by the base player, who is concerned they will never reach his personal goal of making a worship CD that will be heralded throughout the nations. Gina has made up her mind that if she is told one more time that she has to give up her mike, she is out of there, quitting on the spot. As a matter of fact, she is just waiting for that to happen so she can teach everyone a lesson! She knows she can sing better than any of the others. They will find out if it weren't for her voice, the direction for worship would be lost. Tears are flowing with sincerity from Barb, who feels that this team is her lifeline, and right now she needs another group counseling session.

Seeing this from our perspective, it is easy for us to list some areas that are obvious problems. But what is really going on, and how can it be resolved?

Worship Teams Attract Jezebelic Attack

The worship team is one of the most significant ministries in the church. It is the ministry that leads us in worship and worship style. They are the catalyst that ushers us into the presence of God, challenging our hearts to new levels of intimacy with Him, encouraging our faith to believe God for all He has promised. This worship team is not fulfilling their call in ministry. Because they are unwilling to die to self and their own ambitions, they have begun to move in the flesh, giving place for Jezebelic activity to bear its fruit in their midst. They have become dysfunctional.

Worship teams are one of the favorite places for attack. The ministry of the worship team operates within a great sphere of influence. Because of this we need to be on guard, to not give a foothold for the enemy's attack.

The Pastor's Responsibility

As pastor, one of the most common shortcomings of our role in relationship to the worship team is our lack of pastoral oversight. This happens as a result of our releasing them in ministry in a way that also releases them from pastoral care. It occurs because of the uniqueness of the worship ministry and their preparation.

Generally, when an individual moves from the congregation to the platform as a member of the worship team, they experience a separation from the congregation. One of the most frequent complaints of new worship team members is exactly that. They will even reach a point where they begin to look to the worship team as their entire church experience, including pastoral care. That is where the problem begins.

When the worship team begins to view themselves as an entity unto themselves, perhaps not intentionally but in reality, they remove themselves from pastoral care. The longer this situation is allowed to continue, the more difficult it becomes to deal with.

> But when He saw the multitudes, He was moved with compassion for them, because they were weary and scattered, like sheep having no shepherd.
>
> Matthew 9:36

Pastor, we need to give particular focus to the pastoral care of the worship team, with the understanding that by virtue of their ministry call, they experience this sense of separation from the congregation. We need to pastor them as an entity within the body with unique and special needs.

There Is Safety Under Authority

Sometimes we are intimidated by their talent and skill, feeling a little unqualified to address the issues they face in ministry. We even look at their ministry as a sovereign call, releasing them with autonomy to seek God and function on their own. What a tragic mistake! Just as pastors give direction and oversight to other areas of ministry, we must also give that same direction and oversight to the worship team. It's the pastor's responsibility to establish vision and structure for this vital ministry.

This problem has manifested itself to the point where worship teams often erroneously reach a place of knowing that they are more qualified to hear and respond to God and His presence than the pastor is. Consequently, they move from under his authority, sometimes doing this while still espousing commitment to his authority, thereby deceiving not only the pastor but the congregation as well. This is Jezebelic activity.

You, pastor, must take the responsibility to be the worship leader in the church. My heart is grieved when I am in a church and the worship service has started and the pastor is not present to take his active role in the worship service.

A Place Only the Pastor Can Fill

In the shepherd's pouch is the harp or the flute, a musical instrument that, when played by the shepherd, brings peace and security to the sheep. The people in God's flock need to see their pastor participating and leading worship. The fruit of participation will be a sense of peace and well-being in the church. I am not suggesting the pastor must be on the platform with an instrument or singing into a microphone; I am suggesting that you need to take your place in sight of the worship team and the rest of the congregation as you lead by example in expressing your worship to the Lord.

You may be thinking, "But I was preparing for the service ... I was in prayer ... There were last minute things to do." Pastor, I have heard a variety of reasons, but in all honesty, there is no excuse for the pastor not to be present as the visible leader of the worship service in the church. Any and all preparation activities needed for the service should be completed before the service starts.

Individual Responsibilities

Each member of the worship team needs to walk with integrity, giving no foothold to the enemy to bring them to a place of being dysfunctional. Every pastor and worship team member needs to realize the truth of the impact of worship in the church. It is worship, prayer, and preaching the Word that establish the environment of health and growth in the church. You may be sure the worship team will be the object of repeated focused attacks.

> But the hour is coming, and now is, when the true worshipers will worship the Father in spirit and truth; for the Father is seeking such to worship Him. God is Spirit, and those who worship Him must worship in spirit and truth."
>
> John 4:23-24

Let us be the ones whom He finds worshiping Him in spirit and truth.

CHAPTER THIRTEEN

The Intercessors

Confess your trespasses to one another, and
pray for one another, that you may be healed.
The effective, fervent prayer of a righteous man
avails much.

James 5:16

My eyes were adjusting to the extremely dim lighting
as I entered the sanctuary. I could hear people praying but I couldn't see them. Finally my eyes focused and I
saw six people lying face down on the platform. There was a
melodious flow of prayer going before the throne of God.

I had, as many pastors do, scheduled counseling for the
evening in my office. After counseling for three hours, I
locked my office and returned to the sanctuary to find the
same six people still on their faces before the Lord. My
heart was filled with appreciation for these saints who
were taking seriously their prayer life. I felt as though God
had blessed this congregation with a new, intense commitment to prayer.

When Manna Turns to Worms

The time requested by Edith for her and a few of her prayer partners to get together for prayer grew into something far more than I had anticipated. Their Thursday night meeting seemed, at first, to be fruitful for the purpose of prayer. I was continuing to be blessed by this fresh move of prayer when Edith approached me and asked if "the intercessors" could have an all-night prayer time. *Hmmm,* I thought, *"the Intercessors;" now this prayer gathering is a ministry with a name. This is great, I always desired there to be intercessors in the church, and God is bringing it to pass.*

Giving my support to their request, they had not only one but several extended prayer times. Edith called and asked for an appointment to talk with me. "There is not a problem," she said, "I just want a few minutes of your time." When she arrived, she said she wanted to talk to me about her "gifting."

The Jezebelic Attack Seeks a Foothold

She told me that the elders in a previous church setting had recognized her as having a prophetic gift and ministry. She was expressing to me her sense that this was her time to walk forward in this call.

I hadn't known her long, only about a year, and I did not have any particular sense as to whether or not what she was telling me in terms of her "gifting" was accurate. I decided to let her talk and then to tell her that if the gift is there, God will prove the gift within her.

Edith reached into her bag and pulled out several pages of notes from the intercessors' meeting and humbly placed them in my hands. After she left, I read them carefully and felt that the best thing to do was to set them on the shelf and let God prove what He had spoken, that is, if He had spoken it.

Looking to Intimidate

Several weeks passed and Edith scheduled another time with me. When she arrived in my office, I could see immediately that something in her demeanor had changed. Instead of a humble, contrite spirit, I saw a boldness being demonstrated in her conversation that bordered on arrogance. She had another list of things for me to consider. Once again, she informed me of a sense of God's call on her life, only this time she expressed it through her testimony of how He was using her prophetically at a whole new level.

She also felt that God had called her to be a leader, and that this was evidenced by the fact that there were now twelve people in the group that she called "my intercessors' group." When she left my office, I knew I would be hearing from her again soon. Several of these meetings took place over the next several months. I felt my role was to relate to her and help her discern her gift and see her gift used to bless the church.

Looking to Dominate

Then it happened; what was hidden was revealed. Edith scheduled an urgent meeting with me to discuss the ministry of the intercessors. When she arrived I could see she was angry and focused. She came right to the point. "I have been very patient with you. I have given you the prophecies we received over the past several months and you have not responded to the word of the Lord. The intercessors have been asking me why you haven't acted on what we have been imparting to you. I just can't make up excuses for you anymore."

Time to Confront

I told her that it was obvious that this prayer group needed some direction from the leadership of the church, and until we had an opportunity to do that, the meetings of the intercessors were suspended. She said that I was not hearing from the Lord, because if I was, I would realize that they were the prophetic voice for giving direction and instruction to the church. I had only one more meeting with her and that was to confront the Jezebelic attack that was obvious. She and her followers left the church after that meeting. (See "Confronting the Jezebel Spirit," Chapter Fifteen.)

Shutting the Mouth of the Jezebel Spirit

The Jezebel spirit is not interested in spending time in a place where it doesn't count, and the ministry of intercessory prayer does count, very much. My experience with Edith caused me to closely examine how a new ministry is introduced to the church.

The intercessors' ministry in the church should never be ignored or allowed to be autonomous. Either situation has within it the potential of becoming a curse rather than a blessing. How is a new ministry to be birthed in a church?

Proper Ministry Introduction

It is necessary to carefully outline the role and expectation of the intercessors' ministry before people begin to function in it. In reality, this determines and establishes the vision and structure for this ministry rather than the ministry dictating what its role is in the local church.

My confession is that I did not do this well early on in my pastorate. I was more inclined to allow the ministry to bring its own definition to its role and function in the church. As I consider my reasoning for that, my motivation was good. I wanted to see the ministry develop as the Spirit led. However, that development, void of pastoral oversight, is less than what God intends.

As a result of learning this lesson the hard way, we birthed an intercessors' prayer ministry that was a great blessing to the church and to me personally. The ministry was relevant and crucial as the church fulfilled its vision on a day-to-day basis.

Every pastor has the grace and responsibility to be a guiding influence as the Lord leads in the establishing of each ministry in the church. What we bring to the process is vision and structure that is in harmony with the overall vision of the church.

This is especially true in establishing an intercessors' ministry. The New Living Translation of Proverbs 29:18 states: "When people do not accept divine guidance, they run wild." This is exactly what happens when we as pastors do not bring vision and structure to the ministries in our church: "the people run wild."

Like the worship team, the intercessors gain a place of influence as they begin to function in the church. Also like the worship team, they become the focus of the attack of the Jezebel spirit. The Jezebel spirit will try to use them to bring individuals and/or the church to a place of being dysfunctional. In this particular case, the gossip and the accusations were flying, and I was the target. It was being said, "Pastor doesn't hear God any more," and from another saint, "Pastor thinks he is the only one who hears God," and from another, "we saw angels standing side by side surrounding the property of the church, but then they left and so did we," or from another, "God wrote Icabod over the door."

The tragedy of it all is that some will listen and be influenced to make a decision to join the rebellion and become part of the problem rather than part of the solution.

We need to be proactive in the development of ministries in the church.

A Word for Intercessors

You are the most dangerous people on the face of earth, both to the church and to the enemy of our souls.

You and your ministry are so vital to the success of the church.

The success or failure of your role and ministry in the church is dependent on your willingness to be set in place properly in ministry. So many times prophetic intercessors have taken the place of unique independence in the church, removing themselves from all authority and oversight, becoming critics rather than being an integral part of the church. When this happens, you have put yourself in a place to be used in a Jezebelic attack.

CHAPTER FOURTEEN

The Church Leadership

Create in me a clean heart, O God, and renew a
steadfast spirit within me.

Psalm 51:10

For we are God's workmanship, created in
Christ Jesus to do good works, which God
prepared in advance for us to do.

Ephesians 2:10 NIV

A s the soft music faded, the prayer could be heard from
the front of the church sanctuary. The pastor was leading Fred, a young man who was new in the church, to the
Lord. As I gazed at the young man, my heart filled with joy.
He was getting started on the most wonderful experience in
life, knowing Jesus as His Savior and growing in fellowship
with the Holy Spirit.

A Leader Off Course

My thoughts focused on Sid, another elder in the church.
He came to the Lord fifteen years ago, in just the same
manner as Fred. My heart is filled with sadness as I wonder,

What happened to Sid? He started out the same way as Fred and in a few months began to catch the vision of the church and God's vision for his own life. I was blessed as God matured him and he began to move into leadership positions, youth ministry, teaching in Christian Education, serving as a deacon, then to be set in place as an elder.

The looming question in my heart and mind is, *"why has he become such a destructive force in the church?"* He opposes everything about the vision this church is founded on. He has been able to convince a good number of the people in the church that the leadership is not to be trusted. He has said that we have a secret agenda we are not revealing.

I know that the original intent of his heart was to be a great blessing to the church, but now he has become a menacing threat to this precious congregation. My heart is deeply grieved as we face the possibility of a church split. I love this man ... *If only he would repent...*

A Familiar Story

This same story is played out all too often in the church around the world. As church leaders, how do we come to this place? What can we do to prevent this from happening? What must I do so as not to be found in the same place as Sid, that of being a continuous source of division and strife?

Leaders Can Be Used in the Jezebelic Attack

I believe the first priority of church leadership is to realize that they can be influenced by Jezebelic activity. We are not above being used by the enemy of our souls to bring the church to a grinding halt.

I wonder how different the church would be today if we could relive history but without the damage that has been done by church leaders walking out their own agendas, manipulating and controlling others to satisfy their own selfish ambitions. These activities are born of the flesh, and

Jezebelic activity is rooted in the flesh. How much further along could we be in accomplishing what God has commissioned us to do?

Before we swing the pendulum too far in this direction, I think it is important to recognize and thank God for godly, proven leadership that has led with fruitful integrity. However, realizing that the strategy of the enemy is to use people of influence, we can deduce that leadership is a prime target from which to launch a Jezebelic attack. Jezebelic activity is predominate in people of influence and is often seen in church leaders. We must deal with Jezebelic activity in the leadership of the church in the same manner as we do in others.

Jesus Condemns Our Not Dealing With Jezebelic Activity

> Nevertheless I have a few things against you, because you allow that woman Jezebel, who calls herself a prophetess, to teach and seduce My servants to commit sexual immorality and to eat things sacrificed to idols.
>
> Revelation 2:20

This passage from the New King James Version uses the word "allow" and the New International Version uses the word "tolerate." In any case the message is the same. We have a choice to make; in other words, we can do something about it.

Leaders Closing the Door to Jezebelic Activity

Self-examination is extremely important and crucial to successful leadership. Some would say that self-examination is not sufficient and we must bear the scrutiny of others close to us in order for our lives to bear witness as leaders of integrity. I agree we must bear the scrutiny of others, but the first step must be self-examination. The Scriptures speak to the validity of self-examination.

> Hypocrite! First remove the plank from your own eye, and then you will see clearly to remove the speck from your brother's eye.
>
> Matthew 7:5

When we honestly examine ourselves and find we are in need of adjustment, correction, and restoration by the Holy Spirit, we must take the next step. If we do not enter into His grace, acknowledge our need and then repent, we will suffer the consequences of the condition of our heart. The tragedy is, this not only affects us but also the ones we pastor or relate to as leaders.

> Agree with your adversary quickly, while you are on the way with him, lest your adversary delivers you to the judge, the judge hand you over to the officer, and you are thrown into prison.
>
> Matthew 5:25

We are not called to lead the church by fleshly means. Yet, at times we find ourselves embracing means of the flesh in order to expedite what we perceive as His direction and objective. The adversary in this case is the Holy Spirit.

When the Holy Spirit (our adversary) confronts us, we need to agree with Him quickly. The best conclusion when we find ourselves operating and moving in the flesh, giving place for a foothold of Jezebelic activity, is responding to the prompting of the Holy Spirit as He convinces us of our need to repent. We must be guarded, for our own sake and for the sake of the life in the church, and the guarding process begins with self –examination.

Principled Covenant Relationships

There are times when we are deceived by and in ourselves. At that point, self-examination is not viable. This is when we, as leaders, must rely on one another. We must be true to a covenant relationship with one another so that we may maintain our integrity as leaders with one another and with the church.

> As iron sharpens iron, so one man sharpens another.
>
> Proverbs 27:17 NIV

> A man who has friends must himself be friendly, but there is a friend who sticks closer than a brother.
>
> Proverbs 18:24

When we, as leaders, see the flesh as part of the leadership style in one another, we need to challenge each other to a better leadership style. God has called us to a style of leadership established by walking in the spirit and not in the flesh.

> For our boasting is this: the testimony of our conscience that we conducted ourselves in the world in simplicity and godly sincerity, not with fleshly wisdom but by the grace of God, and more abundantly toward you.
>
> 2 Corinthians 1:12

How does one walk in the spirit and rely on the Holy Spirit for all our actions and effort? I have some who say it is impossible. Is it really? Can we offer that as an excuse? We must be reminded that God has another perspective on the challenge to walk and move in the spirit.

> But Jesus looked at them and said, "With men it
> is impossible, but not with God; for with God
> all things are possible."
>
> Mark 10:27

Too many times we offer the excuse, "It is impossible."
In my opinion, that is an immature, disqualifying cop-out.
You see, the difference between walking in the spirit and
walking in the flesh is individual choice. When we choose
to walk and lead the church in the flesh, it is immature,
disqualifying our leadership role. God help us as leaders to
walk in covenant relationship with Him and one another to
be the leaders He has called us to be. Humility and dying to
self are necessary for us to move successfully in covenant
relationship with God and one another.

The self-examination process and the dynamics of principled covenant relationships apply to everyone who belongs
to the church. However, it is even more so with His leaders.

Embrace, Connect, or Move On

I heard a wonderful illustration that so clearly speaks to
the next area I want to address, which is the necessity for
leaders to actively embrace the vision and structure in the
local church.

When you have a team of rowers, and every one of them
is actively rowing, the boat stays on course. If one of the
rowers decides he is not going to row any more, it has a
devastating effect on the direction of the boat. As a matter of
fact, if he stops rowing and lets his oar rest in the water so as
to appear as though he is rowing, not only is the course
altered, but the boat will begin going in circles. The drag of
the oar in the water will prevent the boat from reaching its
destination. The remedy is to take the oar out of the water
and get back on course, in synch with the other rowers.

The sad truth is that many churches are suffering from leaders who have stopped rowing *(no longer connected to the vision and structure of the church)* but are still occupying their place in leadership, which has the same effect as leaving their oar in the water. We need to take the oar out of the water!

Connecting With the Vision and Structure

Nothing can replace the element of passion in what we are doing. When passion is involved, we begin to move through the challenges of the objective effortlessly. We need to connect with the vision and structure of the church with passion. If we are only connected to the vision and structure of the church through duty or obligation, the result will be burnout as we sacrifice our time and effort. When we reach the place of burnout, we become an oar in the water.

Webster's dictionary states that "passion is love; also: an object of affection or enthusiasm." Some would say, "I can't manufacture passion; you either have it or you don't." I cannot deny the truth of that statement, but I do believe you can develop passion by one of two means, and perhaps both should be embraced at the same time.

> For where your treasure is, there your heart will be also.
>
> Luke 12:34

This verse speaks of treasure and heart. The Greek word *thesaurus,* translated as "treasure," means: a deposit, i.e. wealth (lit. or fig.):—treasure. The Greek word *kardia,* translated "heart," means: the heart, i.e. (fig.) the thoughts or feelings.

First, if we are going to develop a passion for what we are doing, we need to make a deposit. We then need to embrace the value of the deposit. This verse states that wherever we make that deposit, there also will be our heart, thoughts, feelings, and emotions.

Secondly, we need to ask God for His passion in our role as leadership in the church. He made a deposit of great value (His Son) in the church and in the vision and structure of the church. He has passion for the vision and structure of each local church.

A Word to Church Leaders

Why is this chapter so important when the book is about "overcoming the Jezebel spirit in the church?" When the church has leaders who are not walking and leading by the Spirit, and who are occupying places of leadership but not functioning as leaders, burned-out and without passion, it is tragic. In that state, the church becomes vulnerable for the enemy of our souls to manifest himself among the leaders in Jezebelic activity. Don't be found just occupying a place of leadership … **move on**.

May God help us to be the leaders He wants us to be, instruments in His Hand, to lead the church victoriously into His purposes in a world that needs to know Him and His salvation.

CHAPTER FIFTEEN

Confronting the Jezebel Spirit

> Nevertheless I have a few things against you,
> because you allow that woman Jezebel, who
> calls herself a prophetess, to teach and seduce
> My servants to commit sexual immorality and
> to eat things sacrificed to idols.
>
> Revelation 2:20

A s I begin this chapter, I realize the crucial nature of what I am about to say. Hopefully, by this point we are convinced that we have no choice. We cannot tolerate or allow the spirit of Jezebel to be active in the church. The problem is in knowing how and when to confront it in order to bring the activity to a halt and minimize the damage.

In Chapter Seven I introduced the subject of the vision of the local church. I trust that the importance of local church vision being established has become a reality to you. In Chapter Eight I introduced the topic of the structure of the local church. Without a structure of integrity, the local church is subject to predictable failure. These two elements in the fabric and design of the local church are essential if we are going to effectively confront and overcome Jezebelic activity.

Discerning Jezebelic Activity

Some time ago, I had the opportunity to see the remake of the movie "The Parent Trap." The story line is about twin girls of divorced parents who have grown up in different parts of the world and suddenly discover one another for the first time at summer camp. It is a very funny and clever movie. One of the main dynamics of the movie was the challenge for the parents to tell which girl was which. They looked identical. The girls switched places with one another at the end of summer camp, each returning home to the parent that raised the other. As a result, the parents found themselves dealing with one when they thought they were dealing with the other. I am sure many of you have seen this popular movie.

Seeing Two Things That Look Alike

Discerning Jezebelic activity in the church is much like the experience of the parents in the movie: seeing two things that look exactly alike, not knowing which one is Jezebelic in nature. The reason for this dilemma is found in this basic truth: Jezebelic activity is rooted in the flesh.

It would be foolish for us to believe that all works of the flesh have ceased in the church. **It would be equally foolish for us to label all works of the flesh as Jezebelic activity**. The church is filled with people who move in the flesh to one degree or another. Recognizing this truth is very important. Jezebelic activity is manifest through people who are moving in the flesh. For that reason, initially it is difficult to identify Jezebelic activity. That is why it is necessary to know how to discern the difference.

Discerning the Difference

There is no excuse for any individual to be involved in Jezebelic activity or simply to be moving in the flesh. Neither behavior is acceptable, and both must be confronted.

Not being able to discern the difference is potentially a great problem. This may be one of the reasons we do not effectively confront Jezebelic activity. They both look the same until confronted. We would rather tolerate than confront erroneously. **The dichotomy is that the confronting process is what reveals the true nature of what we are seeing, whether it is the flesh or Jezebelic activity.**

Fulfilling Our Ministry Requires Confrontation

We have a scriptural precedence for confronting those who are moving in the flesh and not the spirit. The apostle Paul was anointed to set for us the example and instruction for victorious living in the church. In this area of confronting and admonishing he not only admonished others, he also challenged them to admonish one another. Paul sets for us a clear example. The following scriptures teach us Paul's standard and practice in the area of admonishing and confronting.

> Therefore, having these promises, beloved, let us cleanse ourselves from all filthiness of the flesh and spirit, perfecting holiness in the fear of God.
>
> 2 Corinthians 7:1

> Therefore, brethren, we are debtors - not to the flesh, to live according to the flesh. For if you live according to the flesh you will die; but if by the Spirit you put to death the deeds of the body, you will live.
>
> Romans 8:12-13

> The night is far spent, the day is at hand. Therefore let us cast off the works of darkness, and let us put on the armor of light. Let us

walk properly, as in the day, not in revelry and
drunkenness, not in lewdness and lust, not in
strife and envy. But put on the Lord Jesus
Christ, and make no provision for the flesh, to
fulfill its lusts.

Romans 13:12-14

Now I myself am confident concerning you, my
brethren, that you also are full of goodness,
filled with all knowledge, able also to admonish
one another.

Romans 15:14

The Greek word translated admonish here is *noutheteo*
(noo-thet-eh'-o); to put in mind, i.e., to caution or reprove
gently: admonish, warn.

This standard and challenge is especially true for leaders
in the church. Even though Paul's challenge gives a place
for all of us to admonish one another, there are specific situations where Jezebelic activity has been revealed that
require one who is anointed to confront and effectively deal
with the spirit of Jezebel.

Leaders Fulfill Your Ministry

Confrontation is not high on the list of our favorite
ministry responsibilities. No leader wakes up in the morning
filled with joy and thanksgiving over the opportunity to
confront someone. On the contrary, most leaders, even those
who are good at confrontation, appreciate the work of the
ministry most when there is no need to confront anyone.
When we consider how God moved His key leaders such as
Abraham, Isaac, Jacob, Joseph, Joshua, David, John the
Baptist, Jesus, Peter, Paul, etc, we see that confrontation
was a necessary part of the fulfillment and success of their
ministry. Our first example of Godly confrontation is in

Genesis. It was God's response to people who were moving in the flesh and obvious disobedience.

> But the LORD God called to the man, "Where are you?" He answered, "I heard you in the garden, and I was afraid because I was naked; so I hid." And he said, "Who told you that you were naked? Have you eaten from the tree that I commanded you not to eat from?"
>
> Genesis 3:9-11 NIV

Paul, at a very crucial time near the end of his life, spoke words of instruction to Timothy. Preceding the following passage, Paul identifies various works of the flesh in men and gave clear instruction and a challenge to Timothy to exhort and confront.

> I charge you therefore before God and the Lord Jesus Christ, who will judge the living and the dead at His appearing and His kingdom: Preach the word! Be ready in season and out of season. **Convince, rebuke, exhort,** with all longsuffering and teaching. For the time will come when they will not endure sound doctrine, but according to their own desires, because they have itching ears, they will heap up for themselves teachers; and they will turn their ears away from the truth, and be turned aside to fables. But you be watchful in all things, endure afflictions, do the work of an evangelist, **fulfill your ministry**.
>
> 2 Timothy 4:1-5

So it is clear that those who walk in the flesh and not in the spirit need to be admonished and rebuked. Paul's challenge is to convince, rebuke, and exhort. Just as clearly as this challenge is a part of Timothy's fulfilling his ministry, it remains a part of our fulfilling our ministry.

Why the focus on this issue? Often God's leaders in the church today do not consider confrontation as part of their ministry call, or they handle it poorly. They would rather someone else confront so they can pick up the pieces. The truth is, if the one who is anointed for the task of confronting learns to confront, perhaps there would be fewer pieces to pick up. God has designed His church and anointed His leaders to embrace the ministry of confrontation when it is needed. It is key to bringing the church to victorious life. We will never overcome the Jezebelic activity in the church without confrontation.

The Confronting Process

Confrontation should never be launched with a spirit of condemnation. It should always be rooted in love. We can lovingly challenge the works of the flesh in a brother or sister, pointing them to the grace of God Who embraces them with truth that sets them free from works of the flesh. All confrontation needs to begin in this place of bringing to mind, i.e., to caution or reprove gently: to admonish, to warn in love.

Confronting in love begins the process that will prove whether we are dealing with a person's flesh or seeing Jezebelic activity being revealed. The response of the individual will help us begin the discerning process.

The proper response of a person who is desiring to serve the living God, and not self, will be their acknowledgement of moving in the flesh and repentance. Someone whose heart is right with God and who has a motivation to serve Him, will embrace the confrontation with a humble and contrite heart. The resident brokenness will become evident in their honest repentance from works of the flesh. Though it is not always his or her immediate response, sometimes it takes time for a person to work through the conviction of the Holy Spirit, and this is the response we are longing to see. We rejoice as we see a brother or sister move into the place God has for them, even if it is not immediate. I need to emphasize that confrontation, rooted in love, opens the door of the heart for a proper response.

Jezebelic Activity Revealed

When confronting someone who has chosen to serve self — (walking in the flesh out of control)— produces a response of denial or rebellion, we have begun the process that reveals Jezebelic activity. At this point it may appear there is an eventual possibility of true repentance. We should give every opportunity for that to happen. This requires a measure of grace that goes beyond our own, and we thank God for His faithfulness to supply that grace.

However, do not let your optimism replace the wisdom God gives to leaders who are on the front line dealing with Jezebelic activity in the church. We must persist and not relent until we see an appropriate response, or have uncovered the covert activity of the Jezebel spirit.

The Focus of the Attack

When I was a small boy, playing in the backyard garden of our rural home, I was amazed and excited to find a small snake. I later learned from my grandfather that it was a harmless garden snake. But I also learned a lasting lesson that day. When I discovered the snake and picked it up, it turned and tried to strike at me. If I left it alone to go about its business, it would have shown no aggression towards me. But, when confronted, it became very aggressive. From then on I knew that part of confronting a snake was the expectation of it turning on me.

> And the LORD God said to the woman, "What is this you have done?" The woman said, "The serpent deceived me, and I ate." So the LORD God said to the serpent: "Because you have done this, you are cursed more than all cattle, and more than every beast of the field; on your belly you shall go, and you shall eat dust all the days of your life.
>
> Genesis 3:13-14

It is interesting to note that the Scripture identifies Satan, in the Garden of Eden, as a snake. I do not think this is by accident. He is not only identified by Eve as a serpent, but God condemns him to the life and activity of a snake. **When you are dealing with Jezebelic activity, you are dealing with a snake!**

If the one being confronted is stiff-necked, with no signs of repentance, there is a strong possibility it is not just flesh, but flesh out of control, being used to fulfill the assignment of the Jezebel spirit. Take heed, as the focus of the attack is about to turn on you, lashing out with accusations, questioning your motives, authority, and integrity.

You Are the Jezebel

One of the most common retaliatory responses is that you are the one that is the Jezebel (I have been told that more than once). When that retaliation fails, the focus is switched to others in the church. It does not matter to whom, just as long as it can escape the confrontation that has revealed its true identity. It will try to avoid any efforts on your part to hinder the Jezebelic activity (which is to bring to a halt the purposes of God in the local church).

Both the Jezebelic activity and moving in the flesh are launched on the same pad, from our carnal nature. It is necessary to discern and to distinguish between the two, in order to know if we are dealing with only carnal nature or carnal nature being used by the Jezebel spirit. It is the confronting process that reveals the true nature of what we are dealing with so we can take action accordingly.

Consistency Bears Lasting Fruit

Once exposed, Jezebelic activity retreats into hiding, looking for another opportunity to launch an attack through carnal nature out of control. I want to note that often the person involved in Jezebelic activity leaves the church. However, it is important to note that Jezebelic activity does not. It will simply bide its time, looking for another foothold.

> And have no fellowship with the unfruitful works of darkness, but rather expose them. For it is shameful even to speak of those things which are done by them in secret. But all things that are exposed are made manifest by the light, for whatever makes manifest is light. Therefore He says: "Awake, you who sleep, arise from the dead, and Christ will give you light." See then that you walk circumspectly, not as fools but as wise.
> Ephesians 5:11-15

Wisdom Is Valuable Beyond Words

When Jezebelic activity is identified, it is time to exercise wisdom. This scripture speaks of us walking circumspectly, meaning heedful of potential consequences; prudent. Circumspectly is translated from the Greek word *blepo*[1] in the original text, meaning, to look.

We are to walk circumspectly and not as fools when it comes to our ministry call. When we see people moving in the flesh, we need to confront and begin the proving process so the body of Christ may be all God has called her to be.

As we walk responsibly in this area, the foothold of the enemy of our God is dissolved, through the maturing process in the local church. When the church is consistently challenged to walk in the spirit, there will be ongoing progress toward maturity in Christ. When we are dying to self for the sake of His will and His glory to be revealed in the church, the enemy has less and less opportunity to launch a Jezebelic attack. Our consistency in this maturing process produces lasting fruit.

Confrontational Authority

Who has the anointing to confront the attack of the Jezebelic spirit? If we are to be successful in the confrontation process, we need to understand and honor the anointing and authority in the structure of the church. God chooses and anoints those He has chosen for the task.

First, I want to acknowledge once again the words of Paul.

> Now I myself am confident concerning you, my brethren, that you also are full of goodness, filled with all knowledge, able also to admonish one another.
>
> Romans 15:14

By this passage we see that all Christians have a release and responsibility to admonish one another. Challenging others to a walk of godliness and holiness is profitable in the kingdom of God.

However, **there are clearly different anointing and levels of authority that must be honored in the process of confronting Jezebelic activity**. If this fundamental, foundational truth is ignored, the result will be fruitless.

Don't Mess With Someone Else's Anointing

So often we mistake God's grace and liberty as His release to move in someone else's anointing, that is, attempting to do something for which God has not made provision in and through us. A clear example of moving in someone else's anointing is seen in the book of Acts with the sons of Sceva.

> Then some of the itinerant Jewish exorcists took it upon themselves to call the name of the Lord Jesus over those who had evil spirits, saying, "We exorcise you by the Jesus whom Paul preaches." Also there were seven sons of Sceva, a Jewish chief priest, who did so. And the evil spirit answered and said, "Jesus I know, and Paul I know; but who are you?"
>
> Acts 19:13-15

These men were moving outside of their realm of responsibility and authority, as well as doing so without God's anointing.

Who Was to Confront Jezebel

God had a plan to deal with Jezebel and bring His judgment upon her. There are three things to consider in His plan and the execution of it: who, when, and where. As we read in 1 Kings chapters 18 and 19, we see the interaction between Elijah and Jezebel. The battle was between Elijah and Jezebel, so it makes sense that Elijah, or his disciple Elisha, would deal with Jezebel. But that was not God's plan.

> Then, as Jehu entered at the gate, she said, "Is it peace, Zimri, murderer of your master?" And he looked up at the window, and said, "Who is on my side? Who?" And two or three eunuchs

> looked out at him. Then he said "Throw her
> down." So they threw her down, and some of
> her blood spattered on the wall and on the
> horses; and he trampled her under foot.
>
> 2 Kings 9:31-33

It wasn't God's plan for Jezebel's judgment to come at the hands of the prophet Elijah, or Elisha, or one of the sons of the prophets. Why ... because God did not anoint them to exercise His judgment against Jezebel. He had made provision and it would be His provision that would be victorious over Jezebel. Dealing with Jezebelic activity is not a hit-or-miss, let-us-see-if-it-will-work kind of experiment. It is a well-planned strategy, given by our Father in heaven, to provide for certain victory in the church. It is a tragedy when God has provided both the anointing and the assignment and we ignore His provision.

God Provides the Anointing and the Assignment

In 2 Kings we see God's provision for the defeat and fall of Jezebel, the accomplishing of His plan against the house of Ahab, and the specific provision made before the plan was executed.

> And Elisha the prophet called one of the
> sons of the prophets, and said to him, "Get
> yourself ready, take this flask of oil in your
> hand, and go to Ramoth Gilead. "Now when
> you arrive at that place, look there for Jehu the
> son of Jehoshaphat, the son of Nimshi, and go
> in and make him rise up from among his associ-
> ates, and take him to an inner room. Then take
> the flask of oil, and pour it on his head, and say,
> 'Thus says the LORD: "I have anointed you

king over Israel." 'Then open the door and flee, and do not delay."

So the young man, the servant of the prophet, went to Ramoth Gilead. And when he arrived, there were the captains of the army sitting; and he said, "I have a message for you, Commander." Jehu said, "For which one of us?" And he said, "For you, Commander." Then he arose and went into the house. And he poured the oil on his head, and said to him, "Thus says the LORD God of Israel: 'I have anointed you king over the people of the LORD, over Israel. You shall strike down the house of Ahab your master, that I may avenge the blood of My servants the prophets, and the blood of all the servants of the LORD, at the hand of Jezebel.

2 Kings 9:1-7

It is noteworthy that a king, not a prophet, was chosen and anointed to bring down Jezebel. Much to the dismay of some pastors, it is the pastor who is anointed to deal with Jezebelic activity. When a leader is anointed to pastor a local church, included in that anointing is the provision for dealing with Jezebelic activity. If you, as a pastor, abdicate this responsibility, it will be the first misstep in giving over to the control and devastation of the Jezebel spirit in the local church.

On the other hand, if people in the church ignore God's provision for dealing with Jezebelic activity and take things into their own hands, the result will be equally devastating.

It is helpful for us to know the levels of anointing and authority in the church so we can fully embrace God's provision in the church for dealing with the Jezebel spirit.

Confronting Jezebelic Activity in Church Members

The anointing and authority to confront church members rests solely on the elders of the church, not withstanding the fact that the pastor is the presiding elder and the process is under his oversight, with his direct involvement. When Jehu addressed Jezebel, he enlisted the help of others to accomplish what was needed. So, as a unified team, the elders are responsible for the confrontation of the Jezebel spirit in the local church. The confronting should be done as a team or at least with elders standing with the pastor.

Be careful not to try to walk in someone else's anointing. If you are aware of possible Jezebelic activity, don't try to deal with it yourself. Your experience may be the same as the sons of Sceva. Take it to those who are anointed and prepared to deal with this menace in the church.

Confronting Jezebelic Activity in the Eldership

Each local church needs to have those who are called and anointed to speak into the life of the church. I will refer to the people who are relating to the local church in this manner as the outside apostolic company. The people who represent the apostolic ministry to that church are the ones the pastor must turn to for wisdom, counsel, and discernment.

The confrontation of an elder is the responsibility of the pastor with counsel from an outside apostolic company.

Pastor, never confront an elder without counsel, and never confront alone. Have one or more members of your outside apostolic company with you when it is time to confront known Jezebelic activity in the eldership.

Quite often when a pastor is tackling the confrontation process with an elder or elders by himself, it results in a church split. The result, even if it is not a church split, will be devastating to the church. It will also reveal immaturity and arrogance in your role as pastor in the local church. Naïveté in this area will prolong the anticipated victory we have in Christ.

Confronting Jezebelic Activity in the Pastor

The Pastor? Impossible you say, not really. It is with some trepidation that I include confronting the pastor in this chapter because I know this subject can unleash relentless criticisms toward undeserving pastors and their wives. Please do not do that. But rather, follow the rules of confrontation regarding this very important and influential role in the church.

Even though the possibility is rare, it is still a reality that some pastors are involved in Jezebelic activity. The outside apostolic company are the ones equipped to confront such an individual. This is not the role of the elders, nor the members of the congregation, but solely that of the outside apostolic company. If there is a concern in this area, it must be taken to the apostolic ministry relating to that church. It is then necessary to release them to deal appropriately with the matter.

Confronting Jezebelic Activity in Fivefold Ministry

I wish I did not have to write this segment on confrontation, but it is absolutely necessary. Unfortunately, many who are involved as a ministry gift, such as prophets, evangelists, teachers, and apostles tend to remove themselves from the environment of a local church and/or spiritual covering. They feel somehow they are called to a sovereign, independent ministry. This is extremely dangerous to the purposes of God in the church. The responsibility to confront Jezebelic activity in the five-fold ministry would rest with a consortium of apostolic ministries.

Many of these ministry gifts take on the identity of a person rather than a ministry gift. Sometimes ministries are built with dynamics required for self-preservation. The flesh can get involved in the establishing process even to the point of control and manipulation. A heart motivated out of ambition and jealousy will quickly graduate to

Jezebelic activity and ultimately stop the purposes of God. Self-centered attitudes and actions become deceitful, no longer serving the King and His kingdom. This kind of Jezebelic activity must be stopped.

When Jezebelic activity is seen, we must submit it to those who are known to be an apostolic ministry to the body of Christ. Then we must release them to handle the situation out of their anointing and call.

This is one area where we need to see apostolic ministries functioning on a new level. Many ministries are left to themselves, even when there is evidence they are moving in flesh out of control. These ministries are a great danger to the purposes of God when they are not confronted.

The fruit of apostolic ministry not embracing well the responsibility to confront five-fold ministry caught in Jezebelic activity is the loss of integrity. Consequently, churches are reluctant to open themselves up to the very gifts that Christ gave the church for stability and maturity. The purpose of the fivefold ministry will never be realized if it is seen as an object of scorn.

My apprehension is the same here as it is with the pastor and Jezebelic activity. There can be a mountain of accusations based on personal bias rather than the reality of Jezebelic activity. Again, please be responsible in this area and follow the rules for confrontation.

Confrontation Is a Team Ministry

Once Jezebelic activity has been discerned, it is time to form a confrontation team. A confrontation team is the most effective way to deal with Jezebelic activity. During the confrontation process it is important to remember that we are dealing with demonic forces that are led by Satan, the father of lies. He is such a master of deception that he even deceived himself into believing he is like God. This is the main reason not to confront alone.

There are basic rules for the confrontation team to embrace. The team should be formed with an acknowledgment of the anointing and levels of authority. One moving outside the level and anointing God has provided will quickly find him or herself consumed in the process, never seeing the desired result in the confrontation.

Prayer

The team members must commit to prayer and fasting for the team, the confrontation, and the person they will be confronting. I have witnessed prayer totally dismantle the defenses of the Jezebel spirit, opening the door for restoration of the individual being used in Jezebelic activity.

One Mind

The team must be of one mind concerning the Jezebelic activity and the objective of the team. The team must be heard as one voice. The Jezebel spirit likes confusion, and if an environment of confusion is created during the confrontation, it will seize the opportunity for its benefit. The team needs to be well structured with a team leader and well prepared.

Truth

The Jezebel spirit is undone by truth. The confrontation process is completed by the presentation of truth. **It is the truth that sets us free from the power of a lie.** If we focus on the truth surrounding the circumstances that led to the need for confrontation, we will be successful in meeting the objective of the confrontation.

Dismantling the Attack of the Jezebel Spirit

There are many steps and facets to dismantling the Jezebelic attack. The confrontation team must complete the process. Stopping short of completely dismantling the organized attack of the Jezebel spirit is not acceptable, as it only strengthens the foundation of the attack.

Jezebelic activity is a serious, complex attack that weaves itself into the fabric of the church. Its means of progression and maintenance is dependent on spheres of influence. It is necessary to disrupt all of the spheres of influence that the individual being used by the Jezebelic spirit has in the church. The person must agree to step away from all areas of ministry and focus on their own heart attitude and commitment to serve the Lord. They must agree to a set process of being restored to ministry and accountability.

Anticipate true repentance and do not accept anything less.

> Now I rejoice, not that you were made sorry, but that your sorrow led to repentance. For you were made sorry in a godly manner, that you might suffer loss from us in nothing. For godly sorrow produces repentance leading to salvation, not to be regretted; but the sorrow of the world produces death. For observe this very thing, that you sorrowed in a godly manner: What diligence it produced in you, what clearing of yourselves, what indignation, what fear, what vehement desire, what zeal, what vindication! In all things you proved yourselves to be clear in this matter.
>
> 2 Corinthians 7:9-11

When the individual confronted expresses repentance, this is only the first step to restoration. The next step is to see the proof of repentance. This is difficult unless you know what you are looking for. **What to look for must be established through prayer**, asking God for revelation and wisdom.

Diligent Oversight

Since the Jezebel spirit is looking for flesh out of control, it is necessary for the one being confronted to demonstrate a life progressively walking in the spirit. Until that is seen, it is impossible to release this individual from the diligent oversight of the confrontation team.

When the team has focused on truth, the results can be devastating to the one being confronted. Since the devil is the father of lies, he can deceive people to the extent they do not see the error of what they are doing. A head-on collision with the truth can leave them bankrupt of their own personal purpose and worth. As a result, if they continue to stay in the church, it will require diligent ministry as they deal with heart issues in their life.

Demon Possession and Jezebelic Activity

After consideration, I am sure there are some who might confuse Jezebelic activity with demon possession. This would be tragic. We must understand that if the Jezebel spirit is working through the carnal nature of an individual, it does not mean he or she is demon possessed. Someone who is being used in an attack to accomplish the objective of Jezebelic activity is allowing the influence of Satan to dominate his or her flesh. Dealing with the Jezebel spirit working through the flesh (carnal nature) and dealing with demonic possession are two separate issues.

The Issue Is Control

Flesh being used for the purpose of the Jezebel spirit has yielded to the influence of Satan. People who are demon possessed have given themselves over to demonic possession of their being. The issue is control and who is in control. The dilemma is this. **You can cast out a demon but you cannot cast out the carnal nature of man.** The only way to cease the Jezebelic activity is to repent from walking in the flesh. True and honest repentance is as effective as casting out a demon when it comes to shutting down the attack of Jezebel.

Here Is the Bottom Line

We are responsible for allowing the Jezebelic activity to continue in the church. Jesus warns us to take seriously His challenge to deal with the spirit of Jezebel.

> Nevertheless I have a few things against you, because you allow that woman Jezebel, who calls herself a prophetess, to teach and seduce My servants to commit sexual immorality and to eat things sacrificed to idols. And I gave her time to repent of her sexual immorality, and she did not repent. Indeed I will cast her into a sickbed, and those who commit adultery with her into great tribulation, unless they repent of their deeds. And I will kill her children with death, and all the churches shall know that I am He who searches the minds and hearts. And I will give to each one of you according to your works.
>
> Revelation 2:20-23

In this portion of Scripture Jesus confronts the angels of the seven churches. The seven churches represent the characteristics of the church through the church age. It is also interesting to note that seven is a number representing completeness in Scripture.

Ephesus, you have left your first love
Smyrna, Persecution
Pergamos, the compromising church
Thyatira, you tolerate the woman Jezebel
Sardis, the dead church

Philadelphia, the faithful church
Laodiceans, the lukewarm church

Each of the characteristics He points out in each church are all resident in the church today.

Thyatira is the fourth church of the seven churches mentioned in the book of Revelation. It is in the center of the churches mentioned. The characteristic He brings out in the church of Thyatira is very significant.

Jezebelic Activity Is the Central Theme

The central theme He is identifying in the seven churches is Jezebelic activity. It is still the central theme we are dealing with in the church today. My exposure to the church and her leaders, both national and international, has allowed me to witness and testify to the fact that every church has, is, and will be dealing with Jezebelic activity.

Our response to Jezebelic activity in the church must be the pursuit of walking in the spirit, giving no place for a Jezebelic foothold in the church. The balance of the burden that Jesus gives the church is to not tolerate Jezebelic activity that seeks to destroy the purposes of God.

In Revelation 2:24-25 we can see clearly that He has given us this burden.

> Now to you I say, and to the rest in Thyatira, as many as do not have this doctrine, who have not known the depths of Satan, as they call them, I will put on you no other burden. But hold fast what you have till I come.
>
> Revelation 2:24-25

It seems those who have not known the works of Satan in Jezebelic activity and are not suffering from that experience are released from any other burden. The reason this is so significant is the fact that all who are experiencing the depths of Satan through Jezebelic attack do have a burden, and that burden is to not tolerate that woman Jezebel.

There are no other options; we must deal with the Jezebelic activity in the church.

CHAPTER SIXTEEN

Recovery From the Attack

I press on toward the goal to win the prize for which God has called me heavenward in Christ Jesus.

Philippians 3:14 NIV

Therefore we also, since we are surrounded by so great a cloud of witnesses, let us lay aside every weight, and the sin which so easily ensnares us, and let us run with endurance the race that is set before us,

Hebrews 12:1

The letter that I was holding in my hand came as a final blow of the attack of the Jezebel spirit. The letter, sent to many in the congregation came as a surprise. As I read the letter, my heart was filled with grief.

Quality People With Genuine Love for the Church

Charlie and Eva have been a part of the church for the past five years. What a joy to have Eva back into our lives and the life of the church. The Lord bringing her together with Charlie was His blessing in her life as well as Charlie's. We watched them hunger and grow in the things of the Lord. They were model parishioners. In due season, I asked them to be part of a leadership discipling group, and again they shone like stars in the night, shedding forth the light of the Lord as He developed them for ministry. Their love for the church quickly connected them to the hearts of everyone.

Prophetic Call to Ministry

Prophecy had been given regarding the call God had on their lives to become pastors in His church. This word was a confirming word to our hearts and a joy to hear. Charlie began to walk through a year of training, preparing to stand as an elder in the church. Having completed his preliminary training, he was examined along with Eva by the outside apostolic ministry relating to our church. The response of yea and amen from this presbytery was predictable, my having walked so closely with this couple. My wife and I also believed God's plan was that they would pastor in our place when it came time.

We Released Them to Develop Spheres of Influence

Following the ordination service for the office of elder in the church, Charlie and Eva began to function with tremendous fruit in their ministry. We released them to develop their spheres of influence in the church. This influence would be necessary as he grew toward his call to pastor. Their love for the church quickly developed and strengthened their influence. We could clearly see the anointing of God on their lives. Charlie was the leader of one of our home groups and was a faithful supporter of the vision of the church. He soon won the trust of every-one in the church.

Warning Signs Ignored

I was meeting with Charlie on a regular basis for breakfast and mentoring. I had just finished an extended fast, focusing on the leaders and the vision of the church. I sensed the Lord would have me invite the congregation to join in this fast as any felt led by Him to do so. I publicly encouraged any who wanted to join me in their own personal fast, seeking God's will for us, to do so.

My Authority Challenged

One morning at breakfast Charlie indirectly challenged my authority as the pastor by asking what his authority was in the church. He wondered why I didn't run certain things by him. Did I not consider his opinion important? I was willing to embrace the challenge and explained the difference between his role in the church as an elder and my role as the presiding elder and pastor of this congregation. I admitted to him I could always do better with communication, and would make every effort to do so.

The Second Challenge

The second challenge was elevated to a place of correction. Two weeks had passed and he brought up what he perceived to be a serious error on my part. He stated, "Except for personal, private fasting, all other fasting is outside the context of New Testament teaching." He went on to say my actions of opening this fast to the congregation should be followed by an apology and repentance for moving in error.

I was really taken aback by his challenge and attempt to correct me. I couldn't help but wonder where it was coming from. In a matter of six weeks he had completely changed. It was obvious the Lord honored the fast, even in His revealing what was happening in the heart of my precious young brother. Before the end of the fast God was revealing

Jezebelic activity in the leadership. As I shared with Charlie the Scriptures surrounding the discipline of fasting, I could see that my input was not being received.

I Lost My Place of Influence in His Life

It was not long before Charlie was challenging the doctrine that was being taught in the church. He was no longer in agreement with the teaching and practices in the church. He said the teaching of Hank Hanegraaff was challenging him, and he was rethinking everything he had ever believed about God.

After Charlie and I met with a mature brother who relates to us with apostolic influence, Charlie announced that he and Eva were leaving the church. During that meeting Charlie was warned by our mature brother that if he and his wife left the church, he was to do nothing that would hurt or damage this congregation. Since he felt he needed to find another place where he could embrace the doctrine and practice of a church, leaving quietly would be the best approach. Now, just a few days later, I found myself holding this letter they sent to many in the church. My wife and I were not among those who received it.

Squelching the Attempt to Divide

The letter stated that he and Eva were leaving the church, and it indicated there was some difficulty with the teachings of our church. They went on to invite anyone who wanted to talk to them further to call and they would be happy to talk to them.

Up until this point I had not addressed the issues concerning Charlie and Eva with anyone except the apostolic ministry, the elders of the church, and my wife. But now it was necessary for me to address the issue publicly, since they made it a public issue by sending the letter to many members of the congregation. The following Sunday I read the letter to the entire congregation and immediately, without my making any commentary, the congregation saw what they perceived as a deception that had overtaken Charlie and Eva. I expressed my love and concern for them and then we, as a church, prayed for them and for God's grace in their lives.

My heart was saddened to lose Charlie and Eva; I continue to pray for them and have great love in my heart for them. I rejoice, however, that there were no additional causalities from this attack. We did not lose a single individual as a result of the attack. I am convinced it is because the Lord led with wisdom and grace.

Recovery From the Attack

It was time now for the recovery process in the church. My heart was broken as I continued to look to the Lord in prayer, asking what must I do now. I did not want to see anyone hurt, or the purposes of God not realized, as a result of Charlie and Eva's actions. As I sought the Lord, He gave me a scripture to read and meditate on. The focus of the scripture is Elijah's recovery from the attack of Jezebel.

Jezebel Launches Her Attack

> And Ahab told Jezebel all that Elijah had done, also how he had executed all the prophets with the sword. Then Jezebel sent a messenger to Elijah, saying, "So let the gods do to me, and more also, if I do not make your life as the life of one of them by tomorrow about this time."
>
> 1 Kings 19:1-2

The attack had more to it than the 29-word message. Elijah's response after knowing God's faithfulness indicates an overwhelming spiritual attack that threw him into a state of despair.

> And when he saw that, he arose and ran for his life, and went to Beersheba, which belongs to Judah, and left his servant there. But he himself went a day's journey into the wilderness, and came and sat down under a broom tree. And he prayed that he might die, and said, "It is enough! Now, LORD, take my life, for I am no better than my fathers!"
>
> 1 Kings 19:3-4

Elijah experienced his lowest point as a result of the attack. He became completely dysfunctional in the purposes of God.

> Then as he lay and slept under a broom tree, suddenly an angel touched him, and said to him, "Arise and eat." Then he looked, and there by his head was a cake baked on coals, and a jar of water. So he ate and drank, and lay down again. And the angel of the LORD came back the second time, and touched him, and said, "Arise and eat, because the journey is too great for you." So he arose, and ate and drank; and he went in the strength of that food forty days and forty nights as far as Horeb, the mountain of God.
>
> 1 Kings 19:5-8

Even in this place of deserting God's commission for his life, God's grace and care are evident as He fed and cared for this discouraged, depressed man who was in a state of deep desperation. Something within him drew him to the mountain of God.

> And there he went into a cave, and spent the
> night in that place; and behold, the word of the
> LORD came to him, and He said to him, "What
> are you doing here, Elijah?"
>
> 1 Kings 19:9

"What are you doing here, Elijah?" It seems that God
was testing Elijah in an effort to introduce him to the truth
that would set him free and restore him to ministry.

> So he said, "I have been very zealous for the
> LORD God of hosts; for the children of Israel
> have forsaken Your covenant, torn down Your
> altars, and killed Your prophets with the sword.
> I alone am left; and they seek to take my life."
>
> 1 Kings 19:10

What Elijah answered revealed that his focus was on
himself. That is what happens when we are hurting. Also,
what he stated was not the truth. God is about to direct him
to a place of discovering His presence, where he will also
discover the truth that will set him free.

> Then He said, "Go out, and stand on the moun-
> tain before the LORD." And behold, the LORD
> passed by, and a great and strong wind tore into
> the mountains and broke the rocks in pieces
> before the LORD, but the LORD was not in the
> wind; and after the wind an earthquake, but the
> LORD was not in the earthquake; and after the
> earthquake a fire, but the LORD was not in the
> fire; and after the fire a still small voice.
>
> 1 Kings 19:11-12

It was the still small voice that arrested Elijah's attention. Many times, after an attack of the Jezebel spirit, we desire to see a demonstration of God's power as an affirmation to get us back on track, pursuing His will for our life and ministry. God chose a gentle, quiet approach to minister to Elijah, who was discouraged and depressed.

> So it was, when Elijah heard it, that he wrapped his face in his mantle and went out and stood in the entrance of the cave. Suddenly a voice came to him, and said, "What are you doing here, Elijah?"
>
> 1 Kings 19:13

We need to be drawn by the still, small voice out of the cave of depression and disappointment. Recovery does not happen in a cave. When Elijah reached the mouth of the cave, his first steps of recovery were set in place by a voice that came suddenly. God asked him a second time what he was doing there. When God asked him the first time Elijah responded out of his discouragement and depression. *"A bruised reed He will not break."* Out of His wonderful grace He asked him again. "What are you doing here Elijah?" By implication Elijah should be some place other than where he was. It seems God wanted Elijah to see something in his response.

> So he said, "I have been very zealous for the LORD God of hosts; because the children of Israel have forsaken Your covenant, torn down Your altars, and killed Your prophets with the sword. I alone am left; and they seek to take my life."
>
> 1 Kings 19:14

Elijah was totally focused on himself, his sacrifice and suffering culminating in his response, "I am the only one left." Instead of condemning him where he was trapped God commissioned him. **The response of faith to God's commission will set us free from the trap of discouragement and depression.**

> Then the LORD said to him: "Go, return on your way to the Wilderness of Damascus; and when you arrive, anoint Hazael as king over Syria. "Also you shall anoint Jehu the son of Nimshi as king over Israel. And Elisha the son of Shaphat of Abel Meholah you shall anoint as prophet in your place."
>
> 1 Kings 19:15-16

He gave him three assignments that were not unusual to Elijah. They were what God had commissioned him to do. When Elijah was in a place of being dysfunctional instead of allowing him to continue in his despair God put him back to work!

> It shall be that whoever escapes the sword of Hazael, Jehu will kill; and whoever escapes the sword of Jehu, Elisha will kill. Yet I have reserved seven thousand in Israel, all whose knees have not bowed to Baal, and every mouth that has not kissed him.
>
> 1 Kings 19:17-18

He then imparts vision and structure to Elijah and informs him of the truth, which is that he is not alone because God had preserved 7,000 who had not bowed to Baal.

> So he departed from there, and found Elisha the son of Shaphat, who was plowing with twelve yoke of oxen before him, and he was with the twelfth. Then Elijah passed by him and threw his mantle on him.
>
> 1 Kings 19:19

As I considered this scripture, I realized God was allowing me to see the steps to recovery, for myself and for any church that has been devastated by a Jezebelic attack.

Initiating Recovery

To move into recovery, three things must happen.

Recast the Vision

It is necessary to recast the vision of the church. Many times during the attack of the Jezebel spirit, the vision is lost for some and for others it may be clouded by all the pressures of the attack. When the vision is recast it brings stability and purpose back to the church.

Affirm the leaders

It is necessary to reaffirm the leaders in the church after Jezebelic attack, especially if it is one of the leaders being used in the attack (such as in the case of Charlie and Eva). Leaders with integrity bring security to the congregation. Many times the congregation feels insecure after the menacing attack of the Jezebel spirit

Re-commission the Church

The church needs to be put back to work. In other words, they need to be actively serving the Lord and His vision. When we put ourselves into the service of our King, we begin once again to move in confidence. Soon we will be back on track, accomplishing His purposes in our local church.

The Proving Process Resulting in Commitment

When we accomplish these three things: recasting the vision, affirming the leaders, and re-commissioning the church, a proving process begins for each one in the church. Those who embrace the vision, the leadership, and the commission of the church will find themselves operating at a new level of commitment.

When we begin to do the work of the ministry, fulfilling God's purpose for the church; we will realize that we have experienced recovery from the attack of the Jezebel spirit.

Moving On

Rejoice in the Lord always. Again I will say, rejoice! Let your gentleness be known to all men. The Lord is at hand. Be anxious for nothing, but in everything by prayer and supplication, with thanksgiving, let your requests be made known to God; and the peace of God, which surpasses all understanding, will guard your hearts and minds through Christ Jesus.

Philippians 4:4-7

As I sit down to write this postscript, it is after the first editing of the book. I realize that many lives will be impacted by its content in one way or another. It will be perceived and received based on individual experiences in the church.

Some will feel indicted but that is not my desire. If conviction floods your soul, then know this: "He who knows you best loves you most," and He is faithful to forgive, sustain and renew.

Embracing With Love

Some will have seen faces and names as you read these pages. It is useless for me to ask you to please not do that, because you already have. I can tell you that what you see is not necessarily what you get. What you see can be the first step to effective and long-lasting change in the church. I am convinced this can only take place as we embrace His commandment to us.

> "A new commandment I give to you, that you love one another; as I have loved you, that you also love one another. "By this all will know that you are My disciples, if you have love for one another."
>
> John 13:34-35

We are commanded to embrace one another in love. It is the hallmark of Christ's disciples. It is the hallmark of Christianity. I believe it is the foundation for effective change to take place in the lives of individuals and in the church.

Some leaders will dismiss this book as not relevant to them and their circumstances. I understand; I did that for a while. But I became tired of seeing the flesh of man bring the purposes of God to a halt. I wrote this book realizing, as a leader, that it is my responsibility to address the issues of Jezebelic activity with wisdom and a strategy to defeat the attack.

Bound by Theology

There will be those who say the teaching does not line up with their theology. Webster's dictionary defines theology as the study of religious faith, practice, and experience, particularly the study of God and of God's relationship to His creation, and all that it contains. I covered this early in the book. Theology is something we all have, and it can open the door for a fruitful life of ministry in the church and in His Kingdom. If it is faulty it can also be a trap; keeping us from the intended destiny we have in God.

We must not be bound by our theology, so that we do not continue in our pursuit of the ever-increasing wisdom and knowledge of God. We do not serve our theology but rather our theology should serve us as a foundation and guide as we continue to grow and mature in our knowledge and experience of God and His kingdom.

Bound by Tradition

For those who find themselves in a church setting defined by its historical discipline, tradition, and heritage, do not overlook the reality of His kingdom. It does not matter what denomination we have called ourselves. That identity and its disciplines do not deserve priority over our personal challenge to be responsible people in the kingdom of God. We must not allow our traditions to bring our personal development in His kingdom to a place of passivity.

Finally My Brethren...

> Finally, brethren, whatever things are true, whatever things are noble, whatever things are just, whatever things are pure, whatever things are lovely, whatever things are of good report, if there is any virtue and if there is anything praiseworthy - meditate on these things.
>
> Philippians 4:8

Paul challenges the people to a greater experience and a higher calling in his letter to the Christians in Colosse. As I hear his heart to those he is writing to, it expresses my heart to you as well.

If then you were raised with Christ, seek those things which are above, where Christ is, sitting at the right hand of God. Set your mind on things above, not on things on the earth. For you died, and your life is hidden with Christ in God.

When Christ who is our life appears, then you also will appear with Him in glory. Therefore put to death your members which are on the earth: fornication, uncleanness, passion, evil desire, and covetousness, which is idolatry. Because of these things the wrath of God is coming upon the sons of disobedience, in which you yourselves once walked when you lived in them.

But now you yourselves are to put off all these: anger, wrath, malice, blasphemy, filthy language out of your mouth. Do not lie to one another, since you have put off the old man with his deeds, and have put on the new man who is renewed in knowledge according to the image of Him who created him, where there is neither Greek nor Jew, circumcised nor uncircumcised, barbarian, Scythian, slave nor free, but Christ is all and in all.

Therefore, as the elect of God, holy and beloved, put on tender mercies, kindness, humility, meekness, longsuffering; bearing with one another, and forgiving one another, if anyone has a complaint against another; even as Christ forgave you, so you also must do. But above all these things put on love, which is the bond of perfection. And let the peace of God rule in your hearts, to which also you were called in one body; and be thankful.

> Let the word of Christ dwell in you richly in all wisdom, teaching and admonishing one another in psalms and hymns and spiritual songs, singing with grace in your hearts to the Lord.
>
> Colossians 3:1-16

My Prayer

While writing these words my heart is filled with compassion and love for those of you who are reading them. As I lift you to the Lord, I know, in some way, God is answering my prayer for you.

"Father, I believe You commissioned me to write this book. I pray that I have communicated what You desire for me to communicate to Your people. Father, I ask You to cause them to know how much You love them and to know Your faithfulness to complete what You have started. I believe You have condemned Jezebelic activity and You have called each of us to exercise Your judgment against the enemy of our souls. Father, we rely upon Your grace in all that we do in Your name. We rely upon Your Holy Spirit to lead and guide us. We rely upon Your keeping power that will bring us through to victory. It is in Your name, Lord Jesus, that I pray."

May Paul's words to Timothy be our testimony as well

> I have fought the good fight, I have finished the race, I have kept the faith.
>
> 2 Timothy 4:7

Now may the God of peace who brought up our Lord Jesus from the dead, that great Shepherd of the sheep, through the blood of the everlasting covenant, make you complete in every good work to do His will, working in

you what is well pleasing in His sight, through Jesus Christ, to whom be glory forever and ever. Amen.

Hebrews 13:20-21

Endnotes

Chapter One: The Jezebel Spirit: "Real or Myth?"

[1] Strong's 0348 Iyzebel
[2] Strong's 2403 Iezabel

Chapter Three: Seedbed for Destruction

[1] 4561. sarx, sarx; prob. From the base of G4563; flesh (as stripped of the skin), i.e. (strictly) the meat of an animal (as food), or (by extens.) the body (as opposed to the soul [or spirit], or as the symbol of what is external, or as the means of kindred), or (by impl.) human nature (with its frailties [phys. or mor.] and passions), or (spec.) a human being (as such):—carnal (-ly, + -ly minded), flesh ([-ly]).

[2] Proverbs 11:16

[3] Strong's 5590. psuche, psoo-khay'; from G5594; breath, i.e. (by impl.) spirit, abstr. Or concr. (the animal sentient principle only; thus distinguished on the one hand from G4151, which is the rational and immortal soul; and on the other from G2222, which is mere vitality, even of plants: these terms thus exactly correspond respectively to the Heb. H5315, H7307 and H2416):—heart (+ -ily), life, mind, soul, + us, + you.

[4] Strong's 4151. pneuma, pnyoo'-mah; from G4154; a current of air, i.e. breath (blast) or a breeze; by anal. or fig. a spirit, i.e. (human) the ratio-

nal soul, (by impl.) vital principle, mental disposition, etc., or (superhuman) an angel, daemon, or (divine) God, Christ's spirit, the Holy Spirit:—ghost, life, spirit (-ual, -ually), mind. Comp. G5590

[5] Strong's 4561. sarx, sarx; prob. From the base of G4563; flesh (as stripped of the skin), i.e. (strictly) the meat of an animal (as food), or (by extens.) the body (as opposed to the soul [or spirit], or as the symbol of what is external, or as the means of kindred), or (by impl.) human nature (with its frailties [phys. or mor.] and passions), or (spec.) a human being (as such):—carnal (-ly, + -ly minded), flesh ([-ly]).

[6] Strong's 4983. soma, so'-mah; from G4982; the body (as a sound whole), used in a very wide application, lit. or fig.:—bodily, body, slave.

[7] Romans 8:7-8, Galations 5:17

Chapter Four: Modus Operandi of the Jezebel Spirit

[1] Intercessory Prayer, by Dutch Sheets

[2] Strong's 988. blasphemia, blas-fay-me'-ah from G989, vilification (espec. Against God): —blasphemy, evil speaking, railing

[3] Strong's 987. blasphemeo, blas-fay-me'-o; from G989; to vilify; spec. to speak impiously:—(speak) blaspheme (-er, -mously, -my), defame, rail on, revile, speak evil.
Vine's [0987] slander
Blasphemo (987), "to blaspheme, rail at or revile," is used
In a general way, of any contumelious speech, reviling, calumniating, railing at, etc., as of those who railed at Christ, e.g., Mat 27:39 Mar 15:29 Luk 22:65 (RV, "reviling");
Luk 23:39
Rail
To speak bitterly or reproachfully, complain violently with against or at. Of those who speak contemptuously of God or of sacred things, e.g., Mat 9:3 Mar 3:28 Rom 2:24 1Ti 1:20 6:1 Rev 13:6 11 21;

[4] Webster's Dictionary

[5] This is a devotional book written by Dotty Schmitt. She and her husband Charles pastor Immanuel's Church in Silver Springs, Maryland

[6] EPH 4:11 It was he who gave some to be apostles, some to be prophets, some to be evangelists, and some to be pastors and teachers,

[7] EPH 4:11-13
It was he who gave some to be apostles, some to be prophets, some to be evangelists, and some to be pastors and teachers, to prepare God's people for works of service, so that the body of Christ may be built up until we all reach unity in the faith and in the knowledge of the Son of God and become mature, attaining to the whole measure of the fullness of Christ.

[8] Strong's 6680 tsavah
(intens.) to constitute, enjoin

Chapter 5: Warnings Signs of Jezebelic Activity

[1] Strong's 480. antikeimai, an-tik'-i-mahee; form G473 and G2749; to lie opposite, i.e. be adverse (fig. repugnant) to:—adversary, be contrary, oppose.

[2] John 14:26 " But the Helper, the Holy Spirit, whom the Father will send in My name, He will teach you all things, and bring to your remembrance all things that I said to you. John 16:13 " However, when He, the Spirit of truth, has come, He will guide you into all truth; for He will not speak on His own authority, but whatever He hears He will speak; and He will tell you things to come.

[3] GAL 5:19-21
19 Now the works of the flesh are evident, which are: adultery, fornication, uncleanness, licentiousness,
20 idolatry, sorcery, hatred, contentions, jealousness, outbursts of wrath, selfish ambitions, dissensions, heresies,
21 envy, murders, drunkenness, revelries, and the like; of which I tell you beforehand, just as I also told you in time past, that those who practice those things will not inherit the Kingdom of God.

[4] Strong's 4204. porneia, por-ni'-ah;
from G4203; harlotry (includ. adultery and incest); fig. idolatry:—fornication.

[5] Strong's 167. akatharsia, ak-arth-ar-see'-ah;
from G169; impurity (the quality), phys. or mor.:—uncleanness

[6] Strong's 766. aselgeia, as-elg'-i-a;
from a comp. of G1 (as a neg. particle) and a presumed selges (of uncert. der., but appar. mean. continent); licentiousness (sometimes including other vices):—filthy, lasciviousness, wantonness.

[7] Strong's 1495. eidololatreia, i-do-lol-at-ri'-ah;
from G1497 and G2999; image-worship (lit. or fig.):—idolatry.

[8] Strong's 5331. pharmakeia, far-mak-i'-ah;
from G5332; medication ("pharmacy"), i.e. (by extens.) magic (lit. or fig.):—sorcery, witchcraft

[9] Strong's 2189. echthra, ekh'-thrah;
fem. of G2190; hostility, by impl. A reason for opposition:—enmity, hatred.

[10] Strong's 2054. eris, er'-is;
of uncert. Affin.; a quarrel, i.e. (by impl.) wrangling: —contention, debate, strife, variance.

[11] Strong's 2205. zelos, dzay'-los; from G2204; prop. heat, i.e. (fig.) "zeal" (in a favorable sense, ardor: in an unfavorable one, jealousy, as of a husband [fig. of God], or an enemy, malice):—emulation, envy (-ing), fervent mind, indignation, jealousy, zeal.

[12] Strong's 2372. thumos, thoo-mos'; from G2380; passion (as if breathing hard):—fierceness, indignation, wrath. Comp. G5590.

[13] Strong's 2052. eritheia, er-ith-i'-ah; perh. From the same as G2042; prop. intrigue, i.e. (by impl.) faction:—contention (-ious), strife.

[14] Strong's 1370. dichostasia, dee-khos-tas-ee'-ah; from a der. of G1364 and G4714; disunion, i.e. (fig.) dissension:—division, sedition.

[15] Strong's 139. hairesis, hah'ee-res-is; from G138; prop. A choice, i.e. (spec.) a party or (abstr.) disunion:—heresay [which is the Gr. Word itself], sect.

[16] Strong's 5355. phthonos, fthon'-os; prob. Akin to the base of G5351; ill-will (as detraction), i.e. jealousy (spite):—envy.

[17] Strong's 3178. methe, meth'-ay; appar. A prim. word; an intoxicant, i.e. (by impl.) intoxication:—drunkenness.

[18] Strong's 2970. komos, lo'-mos; from G2749; a carousal (as if a letting loose):—revelling, rioting

Chapter 7: God's Vision and the Local Church

[1] Exodus 13:21 And the LORD went before them by day in a pillar of cloud to lead the way, and by night in a pillar of fire to give them light, so as to go by day and night.

[2] Ephesians 1:22-23 And He put all things under His feet, and gave Him to be head over all things to the church, :23 which is His body, the fullness of Him who fills all in all.

3 Strong's Concordance 5275. na'al, noh'-al; or (fem.) na'alah, nah-al-aw'; from H5274; prop. A sandal tongue; by extens. A sandal or slipper (sometimes as a symbol of occupancy, a refusal to marry, or of something valueless):—drysod, (pair of) shoe ([-latchet], -s).

Chapter 9: Stopping the Attack

[1] Strong's 4561 sarx
flesh (as stripped of the skin), i.e. (strictly) the meat of an animal (as food), or (by extens.) the body (as opposed to the soul [or spirit], or as the symbol of what is external, or as the means of kindred), or (by impl.) human nature (with its frailties [phys. or mor.] and passions), or spec.) a human being (as such)

Chapter 15: Confronting Jezebelic Activity

[1] Strong's 0991 blepo
to look at (lit. or fig.)

About the Author

Don Richter received training through Elim Bible Institute in Lima, New York, and was ordained for ministry through Elim Fellowship International. He served on their Board of Administration and various committees for many years. In addition Don has served as a Regional Representative and continues to serve as an Area Representative. Don was instrumental in the founding of Mid-Hudson Christian Church in Wallkill, New York, and served as senior pastor for 22 years. His heart is focused on the ministry of the local church. By God's design he was called out of his role as a local pastor to minister to the need that many young pastors and leaders have for a father in the faith.

His vision and desire is to see every person enter into all that God is establishing within His church. He believes the purpose of God is for each believer to grow into the Headship of Christ, with a mission to fulfill the great commission Christ gives the church in Matthew 28:16-20.

Don is Founder and Director of Harvest Preparation International Ministries, an apostolic ministry network, established in the United States, Africa and Mexico. He has been instrumental in planting churches in the United States and Mexico. He ministers to thousands of pastors and leaders each year in Cuba, Mexico, Ukraine, Russia, Kenya, Uganda, South Africa, Haiti, Guatemala, and the United States. His ministry to many is personal and relational, not only through teaching and training, but through the role of fathering and mentoring as well.

Don has been married to his wife, best friend, and fellow worker, Lois, since 1957. They grew into parenthood with the help of three wonderful sons, Chip, Jeff, and Matt, who have brought into the family two precious daughter-in-laws, Marybeth and Jane. They have been blessed with five amazing grandchildren, Ben, Jenna, Megan, Brittany, and Austin. Their home and ministry office is in Sarasota, Florida.

Don is available for speaking engagements. For further information regarding his itinerary and scheduling details you can email him at <u>ministryrequest@harvestpreparation.com</u>.